12.95

D0546487

ARKANA

SHAPE SHIFTERS

Michele Jamal graduated cum laude from the University of California, Berkeley, in anthropology. She has practiced as a consultant, using psychic and astrological readings and inner mythological journeying to enable others to discover their personal power. She is currently researching a PhD in psychology and writing her next book.

MICHELE JAMAL

SHAPE SHIFTERS

SHAMAN WOMEN IN CONTEMPORARY SOCIETY

ARKANA

NEW YORK AND LONDON

First published in 1987 by
ARKANA, an imprint of Routledge & Kegan Paul Inc.
in association with Methuen Inc.
29 West 35th Street, New York, NY 10001
Published in the UK by ARKANA
(Routledge & Kegan Paul Ltd)
11 New Fetter Lane, London EC4P 4EE

Set in 10/11½ pt Bembo
by Columns of Reading
and printed in Great Britain
by the Guernsey Press Co Ltd,
Guernsey, Channel Islands

Library of Congress Cataloging-in-Publication Data
Jamal, Michele.
Shape shifters.
Bibliography: p
1. Women and religion——United States——Biography.
2. Shamanism——United States——Biography. I. Title.
BL458.J36 1987   291.3   86–28856
British Library CIP Data also available
ISBN 1–85063–060–7

I dedicate this book to all of you who are shape shifters,
contributing your love and life-work to
transforming the world paradigm.
To my mother Anne for her love and nurturance.
To my brother Frank for his loving friendship
and shared search.
To my son Josh whose compassion and humor
has been my saving grace.

Contents

Foreword

Michele Jamal's *Shape Shifters* is a fascinating collection of biographies of strong women from different backgrounds and different parts of the world. They all have creative talents, and all share a vision of healing our degenerated planet. These women sense the divine nature of their femininity. In this I see a link to the distant past of humankind, when both the mythical and the real world were dominated by goddesses and priestesses; when women were not merely "mutilated men" as was thought by Aristotle, Freud, and other philosophers and scholars of modern times.

In her work, Ms Jamal shows us that even today there are women who have tremendous energy and a sense of unity with the life existing in nature. This gives us hope for the possibility of recovery of our ailing humanity. It is rewarding to know that there are women who are not lifeless mannequins wearing masks of unnatural smiles, familiar to us from Hollywood movies and the media, but wonderful human beings who are able to draw a healing energy from flowers and birds, from stones and bears, and from the music and sounds of nature.

The author should be praised for bringing us this vital information and for reminding us that the life energy can be revived, that we can extend our arms to one another, and enrich the quality of our lives.

Dr Marija Gimbutas

Acknowledgments

My appreciation and thanks to the women I have interviewed for *Shape Shifters*. Our meetings for me have been psychically connected, electric, and fresh.

My thanks to the many people who have added their support to the creation of this book: to Dr Margaret MacKenzie, Dr Alan Dundes, Dr Andrei Simic, Dr Marcia Herndon, Dr Marija Gimbutas, Dr Jean Shinoda Bolen, Dr Stanley Krippner, Dr Michael Harner, Charlene Spretnak, Sharon Lebell, Rick Kuhn, Bette Margolis, Abbye Silverstein, Johanna Najmuddin, Nancy Karp, Debby Hotchkis, Jana Robinson, Neal King, Debby Matsumoto.

A special thanks to my editor Eileen Campbell for her attunement to the vision of *Shape Shifters*, for her perceptive suggestions, and for implementing the dream and giving it flight.

Michele Jamal

Preface

Within childhood play, in dreams, and in my womanhood, I've had experiences of the primal, of the numinous spirit of nature. As a creative woman in a computerized society I have sought to find a way to maintain the sacred in my own life and to find a context for the spirit in my work. *Shape Shifters* is an outcome of bridging my vision and work with that of many women who give the primal a voice.

When I was a child, my deepest desire was to fly through the air. I was confused about why I was able to fly in my dreams, but could not fly in my body. I caught bees and rubbed the pollen off of their legs onto my arms, thinking that might be the secret of flying. Once I leapt from the garage roof thinking I needed the extra height to soar. It didn't work.

I spent hours in the summer sitting in my backyard underneath the apricot tree. I drank in the smell of the apricots and ate only the dripping, oozing ones. I in exchange sent my energy out from my body to penetrate inside the bark.

There was a day I went with my father and brother fishing at a lake in the Southern California mountains. While they fished I played at the other end of the lake among the pussy willows and reeds. I had just learned to whistle, and was practicing happily while playing by the shore. Suddenly there was a silence on the lake. The frogs had stopped croaking. The fishermen looked around to see what had happened because the fish had stopped biting. Then just as suddenly there was the loudest croaking I have heard. The frogs in the lake were swimming quickly and making loud plops while coming toward me on the shore. I continued whistling while the frogs hopped about me. To me the interaction was natural, but to my father who raced over to me, the whole experience was confounding. He wanted me to replicate the whistle and to explain what had happened. But I forgot the note I had whistled. I couldn't duplicate something that was spontaneous and that emanated from a knowingness for which I had no conscious knowledge.

I enjoyed playing with other children, but there were times when I preferred to play with my silent friends. I loved the "presence" of rocks. I had many kinds of rocks that I put in a circle around me to meet each one individually. The one I gravitated to the most was a quartz crystal slit into two. I looked inside the egg, holding the iridescent corners up to the sun, and then I placed the crystal against my skin to absorb its cool, soothing energy.

Real storms were rare in Southern California where I grew up. When they did occur, the event was always very significant to me. There was a day when a thunderstorm was brewing. I ran outside, feeling the intensity and blackening of the sky and picked up a stick and pointed it at the rushing clouds. I cried out words I didn't know the meaning of as I felt the electrical power of the storm rush through me.

As an adult I experience a continuity with my childhood, believing now as I did then that the natural elements and animals feel our essence as we do theirs. If we are receptive, we can experience a dialogue.

I lived for a time with a boyfriend on a farm in the back hills of Petaluma, California. He and I were trying to stay in touch with the earth, getting as far away from suburban lifestyle as possible, while still having access to the town. Our home was a renovated chicken coop, situated in the middle of a cow pasture. One day when I was playing a damaru, a small, double-headed drum, I leapt off the sagging porch, and danced in the middle of the cow pasture.

Curious about my movements, and the sound of my drum, the cows came close, watching and listening as they chewed their grass. Their eyes looked heavy and intoxicated. I danced among them, twirling the drum between my hands and chanting the names of the deities.

Absorbed in our play together I forgot about the day when the steer had come after me. They pushed towards me with menacing looks, and chased me out of the cow pasture. Later I furtively ran back to the chicken coop before they charged me. But on this day they stood entranced while I danced and shook my drum.

In my early teens, the Sisters of Charity provided a link to other people who were on a spiritual path. I cherished the time I spent with them, praying together in their chapel and having long conversations on mystical topics.

In my late teens I entered another phase of my spiritual sojourn. I met musicians, poets, artists, and political activists committed to social change. It was at this point that I gained a political consciousness, turning my energies toward social equity. At age eighteen, I discovered that my sexuality affirmed all that was whole and primal within me. The energies between my lover and I were dynamic. All my intensity, all of my ability to communicate went into my relationship with him.

Concerned with social change, along with so many others we called attention to the genocide in Viet Nam, and to the police brutality that was directed toward black people in our home town. The energy our love for each other gave us was directed outwards.

Then the days turned into "the winter in America, when all the heroes have been killed or betrayed," as sung about by jazz singer Gil Scott Heron. My lover was assassinated. My heart an open wound, sickened, I pulled my womb close around me. I pulled all my energies in to heal myself. I spent much time alone trying to get a grip on reality. I tried to realize something other than pain. It took a long, long time.

At another place and time, I chose to live within the cloistered environment of a Hindu ashram. Although outwardly shielded from the country's political and social chaos, inwardly the lacerations were still open. Within the ashram, in pain and in reflection, I entered my inner sanctum more deeply. I was awakened at 4 a.m. each day to the sound of a whispered mantra. Quickly I got dressed, wrapping myself in a sari, dabbing my forehead with clay marks. I stepped out of the sleeping-room where other awakened women were softly chanting mantra. On the steps of the moonlit temple I chanted on my beads. The morning air shimmered with the electric vibration of the mantra. In the suspended hours between night and dawn I felt as if I were situated in eternity. As I chanted the names of God I meditated on the early morning stars and felt intoxicated by the perfume of roses coming from the garden. Within the space of meditation and constant mantra I began opening on a subtler level.

When I left the sanctuary of the temple, a new role had developed within me. Spontaneously I began reading people psychically, and I intuitively guided friends on inner journeys exploring their personal myths and power images. There were days when I felt intense physical discomfort as I felt a searing heat go through my body. Other days I felt extremely high and saw brilliant colors dancing about the room and on my body. It came to me to visualize the colors that I saw spontaneously to soothe myself when I felt stressed or too hot with the strange fire that burned within me. I used the color meditation with friends when doing psychic work, and found it enhanced our receptivity to going into deeper psychic spaces. Later I combined the techniques that came to me intuitively with the techniques that I learned at the Berkeley Psychic Institute.

In my mid-twenties a primordial event was conceived within me. A baby grew inside my womb. For the nine months that I carried my child, I felt no need to practice meditation and no need to strive for enlightenment. I felt full of light. At some moments I wanted to reach inside and touch my baby. I placed my hand over my belly and visualized white and soft gold light bathing my growing child. The presence of the person within me made all other activities distractions from the dialogue with my womb. I had attended school at the University of California the year before, but dropped out when I conceived. I spent many of my pregnant months outdoors, feeling the grass under my bare feet, and the hot sun warming the baby growing inside my belly. I also listened to a lot of music. At one jazz concert, legs and feet kicked within me in rhythm to the sound of drums, and trumpets. Feet protuded, making bulges through my shirt.

At nine and a half months there was suddenly an intense thrust inside my womb. Without thinking, I got down on all fours and began chanting a mantra that is especially potent when entering or exiting this world. The mantra combines the female and male energies within the body. I breathed deep into my belly and chanted out loud. My lover, Rick, drove me to the Alternative Birth Center in San Francisco. In the beautiful bedroom, with candles lit and soft, spiritual jazz playing in the background, Rick and my labor couch massaged me as I chanted and breathed into my womb. The shimmering light of the candlelit room remained visible even when I shut my eyes, and the hours of chanting became suspended animated time. Suddenly bands of energy that I saw in the room grew broader. My friends and the nurse were excited. The infant's head peaked out between my legs. I needed sustained strength to push him out. To give myself the strength to push, I visualized a volcano erupting and the child pushing through, He did not come out. I felt almost a resistance to the visualization. While continuing to bear down, I imagined a large lotus opening its petals slowly until it revealed its full form, beautiful and complete. As I carefully visualized the opening of the flower, I felt a sustained movement inside of me. Then there was a cheer in the room, and my shimmering little boy was in my arms. I cried out with joy as he looked deeply into my eyes with recognition. Within minutes he was nursing. The etheric and earthly connection was created.

My dream-life involved a lot of transitions after I gave birth to my child. The dreams were about giving birth to my power, to my visions.

I had a dream of walking through a Victorian garden, opening iron gates and leaving behind a stately Victorian manor where I felt sheltered and secure. The time was dusk. I wandered through a meadow clearing that looked like English countryside. Ahead was a thick dark forest. I felt "called" into the woods. I walked straight ahead feeling a pull in my third eye. It was as if my third eye was magnetized to something ahead. With each step the pulling became more intense until I was flying head first, moving rapidly through space, beckoned by some unseen force. The pulling current at my third eye was almost unbearable. When the sensation felt overwhelming I realized I had "arrived." In a clearing in the woods a circle of men and women radiated tremendous power. The people, dressed in long white robes, were levitating in many yogic postures while maintaining a circle. I too had joined the circle, and was moving effortlessly into various positions above the ground. A vortex of energy ran through me as well as through the others. Tremendous power surged through my body, yet I found myself struggling to get out of the circle. I was rejecting the power. One thought I had was "What will they do to me for joining their secret ritual?" My next thought came through more emphatically. "You can see them and are part of the power circle because you *are* one of them." Even with that thought I broke out of the circle and flew away into an old classroom. The only other person in the room was a man who looked judicial though he wore no robes. He came to me and we stood face to face.

"You must choose whether you will own your power at this time. It is a universal law that you must express your power or the power will turn against you. What do you choose?"

"I accept my power," I said. Then I awakened. This dream, which I had eight years ago, was an initiation dream. I chose to express the wisdom power within me even though there was resistance. Getting through the fears I had of expressing power would be another initiation.

When I resumed studies at the University of California, Berkeley, I researched shamanism as a system of sacred body-mind practices that create transformation within the practitioner and that awaken such abilities as healing, telepathy, astral projection and levitation.

In my research I read about the artifactual finds of archaeologist Marija Gimbutas at the University of California at Los Angeles. The preponderance of sculpture from Old Europe *c.* 7,000 BC to 4,500 BC, depicting the Bird Goddess and the Snake Goddess, indicates that the bird and the snake were important symbols.[1] The high priestess, or shaman woman, was also depicted as an anthropomorphic representation of the bird and the snake. To me it was clear that the symbols were metaphors for the altered states in which the shaman woman entered. In a trance, the bird woman was able to take astral flights to other realms. As the epiphany of the Serpent Goddess and as a combination of Bird and Snake Goddess, the shaman practiced meditation and mystical sexual practices. A serpent-like energy within her was activated, thus empowering her to experience healing and psychic phenomena. With the opening of her energy channels, the shaman was able to transport herself into shamanic flight. In etheric flight the shaman woman soared into multilevels of consciousness.

When I graduated from the University, that period marked a rite of passage and a culmination point from which spiritual, experiential, and intellectual realizations were coming together. Having researched the prehistory of women shamans, my search for spiritual roots evolved into a quest to find spiritually empowered women who are living and working in our present time.

For many months I travelled, meeting women. Both journalist and anthropologist, I gathered women's oral histories. I was often tempted to open myself to trance and to allow realities to shift in a spontaneous exchange of energies. Along with my tape recorder, I brought with me a series of questions that would return open-ended discussion toward the subject of the book.

I asked each woman questions such as:

- What is your cultural background?
- Do you draw from your cultural heritage in your shamanic work?
- Have you experienced a transformation within yourself at a certain point in your life?
- If so, what precipitated the experience? Example: kundalini arousal; visions; personal traumas; specific experiences.
- What are some of the facets of your shamanic work?
- Is there a vision you are working towards?
- If so, in what way is your shamanic practice helping you to fulfill that vision?

There were several things I hoped to learn by asking these questions. I wanted to know in what way each woman I interviewed helped effect healing and the upgrading of consciousness in those they work with shamanically. I wondered whether there were connecting parallels in these women's lives. I hoped through the answers to these questions that it would be conveyed that there are many facets and creative possibilities in the practice of transformative work. There is a diversity among the women I interviewed in terms of cultural backgrounds and personal forms of shamanic expression. As well as diversity I discerned similarities in personal backgrounds: many of the women did in fact go through many life parallels. What I became aware of through the interviews is that each of the shaman women I met with is personally empowered through the process of intensive inner work. The women share the vision of healing our planet. They are working toward that vision by utilizing their creative gifts, their ability to heal, their personal magnetism, and their leadership.

What we can all learn from these present-day shaman women is that, while some individuals have a more strongly developed spiritual sense than others, we were all born with "primal power," with a dynamic transformative force within us. We can each, without dogma or creed, experience personal transformation and discover our Source by practicing ancient body-mind disciplines, by paying attention to the message within the luminous moments of our lives, and by seeing the ordinary with special attention.

Each of us has the inherent potential within us to be a "Shape Shifter."

By working on an inner level we can achieve personal transformaion. By working on a collective level, with groups, and with a partner, we can convert our energy into resources such as food for the poor, and into healing of the sick. If we put together our hearts, our minds, and our deepest intention, we can use our primal power to shape and regenerate our world.

PART I
INTRODUCTION

The women within this book are shamans. The shaman, or shape shifter is a transformer of things seen, and things not seen. In the literal sense there are shamans who are able outwardly to transform their physical shapes into other forms. Metaphorically, in the sense used in this book, shape shifters can alter their own consciousness, and can affect the shape of consciousness of those around them.

The shaman of antiquity and today is a mystically empowered leader who has done through the process of personal growth and inner transformation. The shaman receives intuitive insights and lives by personal vision rather than by dogmas that are not personally realized.

Inner transformation may enable a shaman to travel within interior planes of existence, to utilize an expanded psychic and empathic perception, and to facilitate healing within her or himself and in others. The shaman is a person whom others in the community can go to as a spiritual catalyst and for direction in self-healing.

The shaman of today innovates change by making her lifework an example of a creative and healing paradigm. She supports herself in a profession and lifestyle that is consistent with her vision.

Each of the women in *Shape Shifters* have a unique and powerful approach to transformative work as they strive towards individual health as well as towards global peace. Each has the challenge of teaching balance and wholeness in a society that demonstrates violence and that perpetuates schisms within people.

The contemporary shaman woman shares qualities with

shamans throughout time and from diverse cultures. She is a "sensitive" born with a predisposition to experience the subtle and unseen nuances of reality.

She is highly creative, working through the media of art, dance, song, dramatic ritual, and creative writing. As have shamans in all cultures, the contemporary shaman woman uses song, dance, and dramatic ritual to achieve altered states in herself and in her audience.

The women in *Shape Shifters* come from diverse cultural backgrounds: from a Montana Crow Indian reservation; from the black South in Louisiana; from Latvia in the Soviet Union; from war-torn Berlin, Germany; from the Midwest; from an isolated ranch in Washington; from the glitz in Beverly Hills; from the suburbs of America.

Although there are shaman women today who are raised with a specific cultural orientation, most are exposed to more than a single cultural form and tradition. Many are eclectics seeking their own way, as they manifest their spiritual work through the diverse cultural forms and inner journeys they have experienced.

Each of the women in *Shape Shifters* has travelled on a rich and varied road. Each has reached deep inside of herself and has emerged with stories of her journey and a vision. Within her sacred herstory she describes her mystical perspective, her shamanic practice, her process of unfoldment.

Individually each woman has gone through personal crises, has faced the fears and demons of her unconscious, and has emerged with an enhanced desire to heal other people's wounds and to guide them through their pain.

There is a seemingly magical initiation process that the contemporary as well as ancient shaman must go through in order to be empowered with psychic and healing abilities. The term "shaman" means "to heat oneself"[1] and refers to the heat of the kundalini, which is the inner fire that transforms the ordinary person into the empowered state of the shaman. "Kundalini" means "coiled up" in Sanskrit, and refers to an energy source inherent in all people. It exists as a serpent-like energy coiled up at the base of the spine, unless wakened by meditation and specialized breathing practices.[2] When the energy is stimulated, it moves along the spine and activates healing and psychic powers in the practitioner.

The kundalini is the power that generates the sacred technology of the shaman. It is the power that enables the shaman to effect the shape of the cultural form around her.

As the generator of women's sacred technology, the kundalini is stimulated within a woman when she makes love, when she experiences orgasm, when giving birth, when she suckles her baby at her breast, and when her menstrual blood flows in cyclical rhythm. The sacred emissions of women are part of a psychic and physical process. A woman'a body is created for transformation: within a woman's womb a child takes form; from a woman's womb a child emerges into the world; within a woman's womb visions can be created that give birth to universes.

Nine thousand years ago in Old Europe (throughout the Balkan areas, the Mediterranean, and the Ukraine) women were the shaman rulers of the agricultural city-states.[3] Within their temples and in the fields they performed magical mind-body practices and visualized the crops healthy and plentiful.[4] They envisioned members of their community as prosperous. The shaman women of Old Europe descended from a much older feminine tradition of sacrality that originated in the Palaolithic period, in which women systematized magic practices to secure plentiful food sources from the plant world. They created magical practices to protect women during pregnancy, and to bring their bodies into balance after childbirth. The magical practices of Old Europe were a continuum of a feminine sacred tradition that was based on growth and nurturance.

The harmony of the agricultural city-states, however, was shattered after five thousand years of prosperity. Around 4500 BC, hunter-warriors mobilized themselves from the Steppe plateau, and massacred the citizens of the city-states ruled by the shaman-queens.[5] They replaced a dynamic life-oriented culture and world-view with one that was militaristic and death-oriented.[6]

Since the beginning of militaristic world dominance, c.4500–2500 BC, militaristic governments, regardless of era, cultural designation, or outer philosophical guise, have had the same world perspective, which is that life was created on this planet for men to subdue, conquer, and when there is resistance, to destroy. The Bible was written at the transition point between matriarchal and patriarchal culture.

As testimony of the new creation, and as the new law of the land, the Bible decrees that from that time henceforth man shall have dominion over the earth and over every living thing.[7] That world view has led us to where we are now, on the razor's edge between continuing militaristic advancement and planetary annihilation.

Regardless of the war against life that has taken place since the patriarchal coup, the heart of the primal still beats within humanity as the spiritual Source which calls to be recognized. As a spiritual technology that incites transformation, shamanism is again being perceived by many as an important transmitter of social and personal change. Shamanism was the primary religion practiced at the origin of humanity, and continues to be a religion of the ecstatic, celebrating our relationship with the Divine.

At this critical time the need is greatest for shaman women to re-emerge as spiritual leaders. The present day shaman women carry the seeds for a future. Women bring our children into the world, and nurture and sustain them. Woman as mother has the personal investment in life to create a future. Women of power are reclaiming their positions as healers of the earth. Hopefully, many women and men will come together in a balance of power, in holy unity to shift the political and social paradigm of the planet.

It is very interesting that there is such a resurgence of shaman women today, who, independently of each other, went through very similar life patterns. As children they experienced some element in their lives that set them apart from other children. They were in touch with a subtle world that was foreign to most of their peers, and which, as they grew up, became a reality of increasing significance in their lives.

Many contemporary shaman women have followed the pattern that has been documented as part of the process of shamanic initiation: they have experienced very deep trauma at some time of their lives from which they have emerged with gifts, such as enhanced psychic ability, increased ability to heal, heightened creativity and productivity, and a strengthened sense of unity with life.

As another connecting link, these women have taken the cultural context which they have grown up with, or have been exposed to, and have changed the material of their lives into something unique and different from the life-role in which they were cast. Many present-day spirit women identify with the shaman women who have lived before them. They feel a kinship and need to communicate about the spiritual and cultural progressiveness of the shaman women who were the community leaders in prehistoric agricultural societies. They feel a recurrent theme in their lives of a dedication to the earth, and experience a divinity in their femininity.

Independently they have striven at this space and time, from a place of isolation as spirit women to a conscious, decisive place of working with others to heal the planet, to heal the people of this earth. What began as an unconscious mission has become a conscious goal to help change a destructive global direction to one that is life oriented, before it is too late.

From this perspective, contemporary shaman women may be linked by a destiny that goes back thousands of years, to when shaman woman were the keepers of the earth.

From another perspective there has been a resurgence of shaman women leaders in contemporary society because of the change in social consciousness that occurred in the 1960s. The development and use of the first atomic bomb had created a pall over the future that mocked life's sacredness. Perhaps as a response to this, there was a consciousness shift that augured the reawakening of the feminine in many people's psyches. Many of the feminine values that had long been buried were restored in the spiritual awakening of that time, and are the values most cherished by present-day shaman women.

In the 1960s some of the women who are shaman leaders today were involved in political activism. Women among them were practicing Eastern mystisicm, others were involved in Native American philosophies and religions. Not all were directly part of the consciousness movements of the 1960s. However, that period is still significant for them because they have found an increased receptivity to their shamanic work due to the ground laid by the activists of that time. They share many of the values, aspirations, and goals that came out of that era, such as the importance of being in harmony with the earth, and of being in harmony with one's own body; the importance of owning one's sexuality, and of experiencing the primal; the importance of social justice for all people, and respect for the uniqueness and oneness of all life; and the need for transformative, ecstatic experience.

The consciousness movement of the 1960s was in part a group of people in quest of the primal, the ecstatic, the sacred, and the truth in all facets of life. The movement focused on "getting back" to nature, getting back to what is real.

People were also going into professions that gave them room for self-expression, and that had a positive effect on the community. In fields such as healing, psychic work, counseling, body work, gardening, dance, music, art, and theatre, people found a compatibility and an outlet that allowed for authenticity and that was consistent with their respect for life.

People began to consciously own their own bodies, creating their own values in terms of self-expression, looking for open, honest relationships. Many worked on shaking themselves from the myths perpetuated by the dominant commercial culture, such as perceiving the body as a commodity. In the sexual revolution, people tried to shake themselves from the psychological shackles of patriarchal religions which view the body as something degraded and beneath spirit.

The political and social movements of the 1960s were focused on liberating people from the exploitation of war, from racism, and from sexism. They were focused on people reclaiming their origins. These issues affected women on all levels: political, social, and spiritual. Many women became interested in knowing about their sacred ancestors. With research into the finds of archeologists, anthropologists, religious historians, and mythologists, women recovered information about pre-patriarchal, matrifocal[6] cultures and sacred traditions that were developed by women. The traditions evolved from women's early perceptions of reality that envisioned all of life as being interrrelated and part of a continuum.

The consciousness movement was in essence a spiritual revolution. Many people were dissatisfied with religious doctrine which did not give them the tools for direct mystical experience. No longer satisfied with an ineffectual approach to spirituality, and contradictory theories, people wanted truth and resolution in their lives.

In response to a growing need, Indian yogis and Tibetan lamas toured the United States and set up centers. American Indian spiritual leaders began sharing their teachings with non-Indians. A new spiritual horizon was created. Eastern religions introduced to the West various approaches to yoga, meditation, breathing and visualization practices. Many women who had had spontaneous mystical experiences earlier in their lives found an enhanced and rapid unfoldment of spiritual awareness with the practice of yoga.

However, there were many women practicing Eastern mysticism who experienced disillusionment when they realized that in some sects their Hindu teachers did not view them as equals, but saw women as the embodiment of maya, or illusion. Within fundamentalist Hindu sects (those dominated by extremist patriarchal doctrine), women are viewed as temptresses who attract men back into a womb repeatedly life after life, causing them to lose their chance to be "liberated" from the earth. There are women who experienced inner transformation by practicing the body-mind disciplines given by the Eastern teachers, but at the same time many women experienced disillusionment, invalidation, and anger as women when they became aware of the misogynistic doctrine of fundamentalist yogis.

Women who were opening to their own spiritual power were looking for a spiritual context for their inner experiences. There were women who discovered individually and collectively that the transformative process they were undergoing was part of the ancient shamanic paradigm of transformation that is two million years old. Many women realized that the reason they were progessing so rapidly with the introduction of mystical practices was *because* of their women's bodies, not in spite of them. The woman's body houses a sacred technology that is especially conducive to kundalini activation.

As a growing number of women are validating their inner spiritual experiences, an increasing number of women are coming to the fore as spiritual leaders in the present time. The women in *Shape Shifters* are among those women.

Although there is not necessarily a singular perspective in the form of their shamanic work, in their diversity and in their similarity the shaman women are interlinked by the sacred thread of feminine sacredness, and by their shared visions of being planetary healers.

As Lynn Andrews says on page 26.

> We communicate without words because the basic life-force energy emanates from Mother Earth. . . . What is beautiful to me is that we can still communicate across cultural existence. I think that's the important thing about the Sisterhood of the Shields. It isn't just focused on one tradition. We really do cross-pollinate everything we have across the world.

Shape Shifters focuses on a feminine spiritual perception that has existed since antiquity, and that persists in modern times. The philosophies and world-views of the women in this book affirm the sacred within women and men, and contribute to the possibility of a society that will perpetuate life.

THE SHAMAN WOMEN

From the primal depths
Life was born
From the amniotic ocean
the womb of woman
the child emerges
From the place of power
where the sperm enters
where the seed grows
the shaman woman is born
She reaches inside herself

in her womb
in her tomb
in the tantric stirrings of her body
there she is born
by the sacred fires
by the sacred waters
by the sacred ether of herself
   She draws up the serpent
   who lives within her
   She draws up
   the serpent coils around her
   and throws back her head
while the serpent fire looks out
through her eyes
the fire of man and woman looks out
through her eyes
the union of heaven and earth looks out
through her eyes
Those around her watch her move
     they hear her sing
     they taste her fruit
     they smell the smoke of her fire
and they make an offering in their pain
    to the mountain
    to the sea
    to the wind
    to the fire
But to know her
    they must know the mountain
    the sea
    the wind
    the fire
they must know the primal depths
as the serpent fire looks out
the serpent fire looks out
of the Shaman Woman.

PART II
CONTEMPORARY
SHAMAN WOMEN

Profile 1

Joan Halifax

*Joan Halifax, writer and anthropologist, is the author of **Shamanic Voices** and of **Shaman: The Wounded Healer** and is the Director of the Ojai Foundation, an educational community.*

My own genetic clan is Northern European: English, French, German, Norwegian. I feel quite close to the cultures of Northern Europe in the sense of their independence and tremendous love of the land, the ferocity of their psyche, their deep appreciation of earth, sea, and sky.

I was extremely sick in my childhood. At the age of four I experienced blindness, and paralysis on my left side. I found myself in the situation where I was quite different from other people.

As a result of feeling very peculiar and being so ill, I had the experience of living on the interior plane for quite a few years. I discovered the world of day-dreaming and night-dreaming. It was quite difficult for me to relate to the outside world when I gained some degree of physical health.

The experience of solitude is absolutely necessary for my well-being. It is important that the balance between inner-time and the time of working in the world be maintained so that one doesn't get too far outside oneself.

In my years as a research assistant in anthropology, I observed that the environmental grey-out of many plants and animals was accompanied by a cultural grey-out of many societies and peoples. My heart was in a state of crisis in the face of the disease of war. Although I was involved in the civil rights and anti-war movements of the 1960s, I still didn't have the spiritual, psychological, or conceptual tools to make sense of this experience of the world.

15

In the late 1960s, I went to Paris, and then initiated field work with the Dogon in Mali, Africa. In Africa many things happened to me, including crossing the Sahara desert, an experience that was a gateway to the experience of another culture, one that was profoundly different from my own. I became extremely distressed about the condition of Western culture and the lack of sacred view in our own cultural experience.

After becoming very ill in Africa, I returned to my family's home in Southern Florida, and in the course of recovery was hired by a medical school to work as a medical anthropologist. In the process of this work, I realized that we can learn from many co-cultures existing with us here in the West. I became a "cultural broker" between various cultures in Dade County and the hospital system. A "cultural broker" is a person who works at the interface between cultures and acts as a bridge. I realized that my foundation in cross-cultural anthropology put me in a good position to be a "cultural broker," because I was aware of the relative nature of the differing social systems in relation to each other. Not only did I not reject Western medicine, I tried to bring about a marriage between the orthodox medical system and the healers in the community.

In the process, I began to experience various sacred traditions. I was just beginning to taste this in my final years when I was at Columbia, and it became a much more personal experience years later. In order to heal the growing pain inside myself, I needed to experience altered states myself. I felt that I couldn't simply record them and then analyze these experiences. I had to participate in order to become healthy.

I had studied song and dance cross-culturally and realized that song and dance can be the vehicles of altered states. One can find song and dance in all the cultures of the world as vehicles of the psyche.

In the early 1970s, I married a psychiatrist who worked with LSD and I began to explore hallucinogens. It was a very profound experience for me. At the same time I was working with people dying of cancer. As my own psyche was beginning to open up, I was with the dying. I discovered why our deepest fear is the fear of death and the suffering of dying. The experience of death became my greatest teacher. In the process I experienced many unusual states of consciousness without the benefit of substances. At this point it is not necessary to categorize these experiences, but they continued for almost a decade.

It was during the early years of these experiences that I looked within the tradition of anthropology to find the meaning of what was happening to me. It seemed that the cradle of the sacred was to be found in the great lineage of the Palaeolithic shaman.

One day I realized that my experience could be defined as a shamanic initiation. I prefer, however, not to define it as that or anything else. I no longer had to consider myself as a throwaway in our culture. It was then that I began to meet shaman healers. At first I felt like a child. I looked into the eyes of shamans from primitive cultures. They were farmers, fishermen, and housewives, and I discovered healthiness, humor, and wisdom. I began years of inner work with the teachers who brought me to nature, to the real wilderness. It has been very, very wonderful to discover in my forties that I have a healthy body, and to realize that the greatest teachings I have received have been from nature, from this Mother Earth.

One could say that I have walked this path with naked feet quite ignorantly. As time went on, I realized that many of the techniques that the shaman uses are appropriate for people today. These shamanic techniques are born of a direct experience of the earth. The shamanic world is extremely stimulating and content-filled. I needed something to balance this experience.

In the mid-1970s I met a Zen master whose dharma was very simple, very direct. I began to practice Buddhism: first, the practice of Zen, and then years later the practice of Vajrayana. Now I try to blend the earth wisdom of the shamanic world with the sky wisdom of the Buddhist world.

Things become simple when you have a taste of both the Absolute and the richness of the relative truth. There, between these two truths, one finds the path of the "Awakening Warrior." One realizes that one is not simply to be a solitary realizer just to obtain simplicity and some degree of luminosity for oneself. One should also help other people to work in the world in a good way, and do whatever one can to foster harmony and beauty, and try to help reduce the complexity. Having been with different teachers as student, friend, and co-teacher, I find myself interested in appreciating everyday existence and trying to foster that appreciation in others.

There is a trap in the extraordinary. One begins to feel special and self-important, along with an absence of compassion. Maybe it is disappointing, this talk of simplicity in favor of the more dramatic aspects of being shaman. What we all want at our core is to be free from suffering; we want to be in a situation of simplicity. We don't want to be driven by desire, or hate; nor do we wish to be caught in confusion. Moving past these three poisons means that we discover simplicity, harmony, relaxation, compassion, and wisdom. From this awakening arises the impulse to help others.

Years ago when I was in a state of acute suffering, part of the release from the conditioning of my past involved the opening of a desire to heal others. Later, in the 1970s and early 1980s much time was devoted to the healing of my own body. In the summer of 1984, however, a shift occurred. I went hiking in the Swiss Alps with a friend. When we reached a place where we were going to stay, at three o'clock in the morning, he was in extreme physical pain. His lower back was in a severe spasm.

Although I had not done any laying on of hands for many years, I realized that since our friendship was very subtle yet uncomplicated, I loved him unconditionally. Suddenly something happened inside my belly, my heart, and my hands; I knew that I could help facilitate his healing. He was in such difficulty that he could neither walk nor stand. So I began to work on his body. It was as though I were guided by his condition to do exactly what needed to be done.

I cannot begin to tell you how deep this feeling was for me. In part it was because of the simple nature of our relationship and in part it was because of my work with people dying of cancer. I could love dying people unconditionally. How could there be conditions since I realized how important our relationship was? I realized that there was nothing that I could expect from that friendship except what was happening at that very moment. Thus, I was able to give away everything that blocked my helping him. For several hours I worked and then I realized that what I experienced in that interaction was something that could inform my relationships with all beings.

An aspect that calls to be examined in our lives now has to do with the feminine and the earth. We need to look at our role as women in relation to helping people in our culture to discover the extraordinary beauty of the earth. Part of this has come about for me because I have made a friend of my womanhood. I've discovered my woman shield to be deep and profoundly creative. I am not afraid of my woman. I have a strong sense of great joy at being her. By the same token, I have a strong relationship with my man shield, the healer.

There has been a weaving together of sky consciousness with earth consciousness. I feel healed intellectually with the gift of Buddhism and from the experience of the shaman. The earth has healed my body.

Now I am bringing a sense of equanimity and harmony between these pairs of opposites to others. It is not so much as something to teach, but as something to be. Those who walk in the wilderness will sense that balance directly. One feels no need to built statues to the goddess. One can sit under a tree. One feels no need to create a throne for her to sit on. Her throne is everywhere on this earth.

Profile 2

Lynn Andrews

Lynn Andrews is a shaman woman trained by the Manitoba medicine women. She is the author of **Medicine Woman**, *which is soon to be released as a film,* **Flight of the Seventh Moon**, *and* **Jaguar Woman**. *Her books describe her shamanic initiation, her extraordinary experiences, and her visions. Lynn practices one-to-one shamanic counseling and lectures throughout the country.*

I was raised on a ranch in Washington outside of Spokane. I had a tremendous connection with the earth, a feeling for the animals and for the life in plants and trees. I was lonely as a child but I sensed some kind of destiny, although I didn't have a clue of what that was. My first friend and I would get on our horses at about 4.30 in the morning and together we would ride in one direction all day, never meeting anyone else along the way.

I have always loved to write, and have kept a journal since I was a child. When I was six years old I was writing horse stories and articles for children's magazines.

When I was fourteen I moved with my family to LA. I was having psychic experiences at that time and thought that there must be something wrong with me. I could see lights around people and I was having a lot of visionary dreams.

My mother was wonderfully supportive of me in a lot of ways but she didn't really understand what was doing on with me. My father did understand but we were estranged at that point since my parents were divorced.

As a result of not knowing myself I went into a life that was completely wrong for me. I went to college and studied philosophy, then after college I became a stockbroker. I was

21

aimless, not knowing what my focus was. I got married and had a child. Later I became involved in films. The film people were lovely, but I just couldn't resonate with them.

Towards the end of my twenties, I couldn't define myself as a woman at all. I only knew what it was that I didn't want. Finally, through a series of extraordinary visions and experiences, I met my spiritual teacher, an Indian Medicine Woman named Agnes.

Before I met Agnes I was at a point where I didn't know whether or not I wanted to live, though I did not want to commit suicide. I just did not see a reason for living. I felt a tremendous pain in myself, in the world, and in relationships. The emptiness of most people's lives was so incredibly evident to me, as was the emptiness in my own life. I accomplished a lot but I didn't know where it fit into the scheme of things. I did know, however, that there was something in life that I was totally missing, and that I couldn't see with ordinary vision.

When I met Agnes I saw something in her that I knew I needed to be a total woman. I had not found that anywhere before. I could see true power in her. When one comes face to face with true power in an enlightened being – it's irresistible.

Agnes creates situations in which I learn from direct experience. Her teachings are not borrowed knowledge. Agnes sees where I am losing spirit energy. She knows what I need.

For instance, when I came to see her, she said, "I want you to write the first of the four books about this teaching. Don't return until it's finished." I had never written a book and I was frightened. But I wrote that first book because I knew that otherwise I couldn't see her. She didn't tell me then that I had to work on my masculine side. She didn't say to me, "You are so much in the feminine, so much into contemplation, and so much in the west, in the medicine world – you need to develop your masculine side." I developed those aspects of myself by writing those books.

For women in particular, and for men also, it is very important to make an act of power. Agnes told me to write my book. I thought she wanted me to write a book about her teaching. But what she was really asking me was to make an act of beauty, an act of power, a mirror of who I am. How do you see who you are? You have to create something in the world that shines back when you look at yourself.

Agnes said something quite wonderful. She said, "We come into this earth plane like a piece of smashed mirror. Each piece reflects the light of the Great Spirit. Because it is a smashed mirror, we're in fragments. In the process of putting those fragments together, like pieces of a puzzle, we are able to learn our life lessons."

The process of the "shields" is exactly like that. It's putting the fragments together into a working shield or mandala that you hold up in life and say, "This is who I am, as a woman or as a man."

I think that what my work is about is to help women understand that we come to this earth plane, onto a female earth. Women come onto this earth with an inner knowing. They have an innate understanding of the earth even if they cannot define that understanding. Men come onto the earth not knowing, and they are desperately seeking a teacher. When a man meets a woman he tests her without even realizing it. He wants to know: "Are you a Goddess for me, able to lead me out of the darkness?"

I found that all energy is the same but that our translations of it are different. A woman translates the earth energy differently than a man. So you have to deal with what a woman is, and what a man is, though the life-force is the same in all living things. Women have to be taught differently from men, and men don't necessarily understand that.

The problem is that this society has taught women to not take their own power. Women have to turn that around, take the power, and teach men how to live. Women need to be able to give that gift to men, so that men can give back other gifts to women. Then the balance is restored.

We have lost our sense of sacredness in this society. We think of God and the Goddess as outside ourselves. I'm always amazed when people come to me and talk about the Goddess as if I'm not one! Who do they think the Goddess is? She's you! She's me!

It's very hard for women to own that they have that power since women have always been taught not to take their power.

But the most important thing to realize is not the Goddess, and not God exclusively, but the balance of the two. The masculine is important as well as the feminine. If we destroy one we destroy ourselves.

When I was teaching classes, I looked around at all those people in front of me and realized I was giving the same medicine to everyone. Each person is unique. Agnes told me in the very beginning that our whole educational system is built upon a body of knowledge. We sit, we listen, we memorize, we take notes, but we don't know how to implement that knowledge in our daily lives.

Now I no longer teach classes, but work on a one-to-one basis, and teach each person on an experiential level. For example, if I talk about the power held in my throat, I can teach how to let that energy go by making a throat bundle – doing something that is external and tangible to see what you are doing to yourself.

The reason that I teach shamanism is because psychology doesn't really teach you to be your own teacher. I think that we have to look deeply within ourselves to that still point, to begin to see our own reflections and study them.

What I do is take people down to the essence. I look at all the layers of conditioning, like layers of an onion. I tear the layers down so that you can get down to what you're really afraid of. Otherwise with all the covering you don't have a chance to see the world as it really is. The vision is veiled. The process of enlightenment is tearing the veils away.

I also help people to understand that they have to be balanced with good fitness on a physical level. You really have to take care of your body. You have to feed this lodge properly, and listen to how your body feels. If your body isn't feeling great you're going to have a hard time, because a lot of what you learn in "realization" and in shamanism is in your body.

My own dream includes working with sweet medicine and working with the animals. I feel human beings owe a tremendous amount to the animal kingdom. If we stop slaughtering animals in an unconscious way perhaps we can stop killing each other. One of my dreams is to have a wildlife preserve, or help a wildlife preserve that has endangered species.

There is a woman named Linda Tarkington Jones who is practicing Feldenkrais (a process of pressure and visualization) on horses and other animals. Because animals think in pictures, you can learn to throw the pictures back and forth with them to communicate. Linda has just come from Russia where she had a chance to work with the cavalry horses on the Olympic team. She's trying to initiate a TV special, airing from Russia and the US, showing the communication between animals.

I think it's very important to study psychic research. If we could start communicating on these levels, perhaps we could cross over political lines.

Our way of life is presently destroying the earth as we know it. We all know this. This earth is a schoolhouse. I don't think the universe wants to lose this "schoolhouse." We're all here to learn, and all the things going on right now are things that we all need to know. We're learning about our own violence. The human being is very violent. Our violence has to do with our fear and our total ignorance.

Women in particular need to support each other. When I see another woman trying to destroy her sister, I wonder about the woman. If we understand each other, we should meet each other and try to come to some understanding. We need to get back to the circle where each person is sacred.

The Sisterhood of Shields brought into reality the idea that we are all from different parts of the world, and that we should honor each other. We are each trying to bring that about on the earth in some way. We are all working in different ways, and in different areas.

The Sisterhood of Shields is a secret society of women who work towards self-realization. The society is based on the ancient traditions of women. Although originally the members were all Native Americans, because of the needs of the time, women of other races are now initiated into the Sisterhood. As we share our wisdom we help bring a balance to the planet.

The Sisterhood has a connection with the dolphins, and even with Sirius the dog star. There is a great link between the native world, the Pleiades, and the Milky Way. Almost without exception every native tradition has some reference to the Seven Sisters. In our initiations it is very important that the Pleiades are directly overhead.

There are a lot of things that I allude to simply because I can't explain them directly. In my books, however, there are guideposts, marks along the way. If you can see them and pick them up, you can follow the trail.

The interesting thing to me is that in all native traditions, whether from Australia, Africa, Canada, or the Yucatan, the language is the same.

We communicate without words because the basic life-force energy emanates from Mother Earth. You can translate it in various ceremonies that are vastly different from one another, but the energy is still the same. What is beautiful to me is that we can still communicate across cultural existence. I think that's the important thing about the Sisterhood of Shields. It isn't just focused on one tradition. We really do cross-pollinate everything we have across the world.

Profile 3

Luisah Teish

*Luisah Teish is the author of **Jambalaya: The Natural Woman's Book of Personal Charms and Practical Rituals**. She is voudou High Priestess — a Mother of Spirits. She is a healer, story-teller, dancer, and is currently teaching African Dance at the* Institute for Culture and Creation Spirituality *at Holy Names College in Oakland, California.*

In my tradition, I would be called a "mother of the spirits." I belong to a class of priests and priestesses who have successfully completed an initiation and are going through continuous training in order to hone and eventually perfect channel information that comes from the consciousness of our ancestors, which we call Eguns, and the consciousness of the forces of nature, which we call Orishas.

An Egun is the consciousness of a spirit that has lived before. The consciousness of the forces of nature, the ocean, wind, fire, etc., are called Orishas, which means owners of the head. So the Orisha that owns your head speaks to the primary natural attribute: the primary power that makes up your personality, and your particular path.

I would have to call myself one who is born out of the Afrodiasporic tradition. My grounding is in the tradition of voudou in New Orleans.

I think my biggest goal is to offer other people a perspective on things. When you belong to a religion that has been pressed down and denigrated for so long, there is a tendency in the early years to be defensive. When I studied religion in college it drove me crazy that Christianity, Judaism, Buddhism would be presented as the major world religions. Then when they talked about African religion we had this crazy little title called animism, or fetishism.

There comes a time when you have to say that this classification is not correct. Then you go beyond anger to understanding that it really is important for the people, the masses at a grass-roots level, to understand that they have access to all the power. We can reach out and put our power in the universe. It does not belong to one class of people or another, and is available for all of us, if the cape of obscurity is removed. Each of us can come to understand that we are a cell in the body of the Almighty. Therefore from before conception we each have a certain amount of power that is accessible to us.

The word "voudou" inspires fear in most people. This has come from a lack of proper definition of the word. If we go to the Fon people of Africa, the word means creative genius and protective spirit. Voudou also means foresight – that which is inherently known. But we get a negative association because when black people were enslaved one of the justifications of the "anti-Christ" behavior of the slavers was to say they had to "turn savages into civilized Christians."

One of the things that prompted me to embrace West African tradition was my encounter with the sky deity, whom we call Obatala. It comes from *oba*, or king, and *tala*, a particular kind of white cloth. We refer to Obatala most often as Ba–ba or father; Obatala sometimes shows up in folklore as a male, sometimes as a female, and sometimes as a consort.

As a child I had serious problems with the Christian God. First of all he was a white man: I grew up in the pre-integrated black South. When I looked around me – you know – hey! This is cracker time! I'm supposed to spend my time on my knees praying to a cracker?! Give me a break! He was this great bearded dude in the sky who didn't hear people's petitions, who had cast me into slavery because I was black, and who had me inferior because I was a woman. Right?!

What most people think of as the Great Gift terrified the hell out of me. This dude had his only child killed! When I started looking at him I said, "Hey, boyfriend, I've got a lot of problems with *you*." I tried in typical Virgo fashion to emotionally approach this God. He didn't answer any of my petitions. I couldn't understand why this fellow who's supposed to be all good allowed the devil to exist and allowed these things to go on.

Finally I turned away from dealing in heart at all with the divine father. I got to a place where I used to shake my fist at the sky. I found my greatest help and encouragement in the Virgin Mary. In Mommy.

When I first stumbled upon some real understanding of West African theology it wasn't a head trip, it was through dance. It was something I felt in my body, something that moved me, something that possessed me before I began to analyze it.

At the time I had no knowledge of the language, just random tales coming past me. One of the beautiful tales was that in the beginning there was only Olodumane. Then we started to get other gods that represent the clouds, the sun, the moon, and so on. Then we come to Obatala, who, upon seeing the rest of creation, decided that something was missing, and decided to create humans.

In the creation of humans, She made a few first and was so pleased with what She had done, that She tapped Herself a jug of palm wine from a tree and celebrated! She drank some and created some more, got sloppy drunk, fell asleep and then made a mistake.

Now while Obatala was asleep, those clay models were laying down there. The Breath came along and entered them and gave them life. When Obatala awoke and saw what She had done, She thought, "Oh wow! I've really blown it!" In the original folklore She made hunchbacks, cripples, crazies: some blind, some deformed in different ways. That has to be extended to problems of spirit and personality, and suffering.

The nature of Obatala is such that when the complaint was, "I made a mistake," the Breath said, "Yea, but that's your project. I just did my part. I just blew my breath in and said, 'Baby, this is yours!' You do with it as you will. You can destroy it if you want to." Mommy said, "I'm not *that* kind of Goddess." What She did instead was give us room to be imperfect. In fact, in certain places in Nigeria, people like hunchbacks, cripples, albinos, etc., are considered sacred to Obatala. Our deities are very human. I can live with them. I go to my altar and say, "Obatala, I made a mistake." Without fear of being condemned to fire and brimstone, I can be given another opportunity to deal with.

The story of Obatala made me cast my eyes to the sky without balling up my fists. It made me able to reach out an open hand and say, "Here's somebody I can relate to." It makes all the difference in the world. Obatala is *wonderful*!

The entire pantheon is so human that you don't feel like you are bowing to a superior. You feel like you have a relative or a friend with *extra* human powers who can help you. A relationship is established when you are not just a peon dragging the floor in front of them. It has saved my physical life and my sanity and has made me feel better about being a human being. Unlike other religions you can be involved in anything else that you want to. Whatever we run into we welcome it as already ours, and welcome it into the clan.

This drives Christian missionaries in Africa crazy because they go in with absolute Jesusism. The Africans look at Jesus and they say, "Well, he's a good boy; he was crucified; he did healing; he was merciful; ah! . . . . this is the son of Obatala." They "pick Jesus up," put him on Obatala's altar and say, "Welcome home, son."

We do the same thing with people. If you would have attended the feast we had two weeks ago you would have met black Americans, white Americans, and a sister who is Filipino. The only criterion for whether or not you can be in this religion is which Orisha claims your head during the question asked.

We have an oracle that is composed of a set of cowrie shells. When a person feels that they are interested in voudou, the shells are asked, "Whose child is this?" The oracle is called Dilloggun – "one who reads time."

I'm a reader's reader! I love tarot cards, water gazing, bones, stones, coffee-leaves, tea-leaves. I love the Dilloggun, because with it you can read a person's past, present, and the general trends of one's future. You can give them a set of folk-tales that they ought to meditate on.

For every problem that the oracle speaks of, there's a prescription for the remedy. According to the number of shells that fall female side up, the oracle is saying, "This person is a daughter of the ocean," or "this person is the daughter of the river," You belong to a particular element and a particular deity.

I have seen occasions when the shells were thrown, and the reader said to the person, "You're welcome to come to our ceremonies, I will do a certain kind of work for you, but you really belong to a Buddhist tradition." But whether or not you are admitted into a congregation is not based on what race you are. We're a rainbow. In fact there are a lot of interracial marriages in our tradition.

Once you join we become like a family. We have houses and families. You'll find all kinds of people who become related to each other in this tradition.

There's a popular myth that this is a religion of the poor and ignorant. I'm not at liberty to expose these people's names, but I can tell you there are politicians and movie stars, nurses and doctors, scientists, and maids: we run the gamut.

I feel myself to be somebody who is always going through various transformations. But of the two that stand out the most in my mind, one was in the winter of 1974. I call it the "needy winter," and I was so alienated and arrogant. A number of things happened to me. I had a baby that lived twelve hours and died. Two of my dance partners had died: one in an accident, one to illness, I'd been taking doctor-prescribed dope – valium. You go to the doctor, the doctor slips you some Quaalude; after a while you're taking all kinds of approved poison.

I was tired of hearing that my music was jackass music, that my kind of dance was inferior hip-shaking dance. I was tired of hearing various black and white versions of female inferiority. There's white on black racism, and then there's black on black sexism. People would like to say that one hurts more than the other. But that's hard for me to say because I've suffered both at the same time, and found it a deadly combination. A black woman under those circumstances is nobody, with nothing to do, nowhere to go, except one form of slavery or another.

It seemed to me to have started one day when I looked out my window and the wind was blowing the grass in the direction of the east and I wanted it to blow in the direction of the west. I decided that there was a conspiracy against me, because the wind was not blowing the grass the way I wanted it to go. When I heard myself say it, I said, "Teish, something's wrong." That started off a whole chain of events where I started to perceive myself in a way that made me arrogantly say, "Hey, I'm a captive on this planet. I didn't create these conditions that I'm living under. I may not have any power over anything else but I can tip out of here. I don't *have* to stay. And behind that I took a random handful of these pills that the doctors had given me, wrote a note to my sister saying, "See you later, kid," and swallowed them – ceremoniously lay down in my bed and said, "Good-bye, I'm checking out. Good-bye, cruel world."

Instead of "checking out" I had an experience where a paper-thin image of me rose up out of my body and sat on the ceiling connected at the heart chakra by a thin blue cord.

She sat up there and had an argument with the body lying on the bed. She up there saw the one on the bed adopt the appearance of death: greyish skin, lips and eyes sealed, no breathing. But this argument went on between body and soul, where body said, "I cannot endure any more." Soul argued in favor of enduring. The final message was, "Get back in your body, girl; you have work to do. Your only problem is fear. Decide now that you will *fight* – because you will *not* die."

I can remember returning to my body and then having a whole room filled with visions, filled with these words of instruction, of work that I have to do. I went into what seemed like a real deep sleep. The way my memory puts it to me, what sparked the coming together of body and soul was that my younger sister who was living with me came and touched my body. When she touched it I wanted to tell her, "There's nobody there."

I can't explain why, but she needed something, and her needing something made me want to get back in my body so I could give her what she needed. That's just the catalyst. I could clearly see the assignments about what I had to do. The crux of it was that I had to fight for my rights as a black, as a woman, as a spiritual person, and not necessarily in approved, popular ways.

When I talk about the "me" that I was before that experience, I find myself saying "she," a third person. I understand that it's my personal history. It's not like a slate was wiped clean, but everything that had plagued me before has been turned into *compost* out of which the new me was growing. I feel that in some ways I'm on automatic pilot. I go from day to day, living my life and doing what I see to be right, and then, Snap! "You're living the vision, kid – this is a scene from the big picture. I'm on."

What it has done for me – it's taken me from being someone who found my life tolerable at best, to somebody who can say, "Even when I'm broke, even when I'm sick, even when the people I care about most are mistreating me or misunderstanding me, when the political situation is crummy, and there's steam coming out of my nose, no matter what's going on – I may bitch and complain and fight, but there's still a place I can say, 'I *love* my life.' "

I *like me*. I'm happy to be alive. I know that I'm important. I can't trade that. I can't think of anything that I would trade for.

Prior to that time I had been somebody who had studied African religion, who had been initiated in the sun worshipper's temple, and did the dances of these gods, and these Orishas. I wore the clothes and the jewels. But when I shared that experience with a man that I know, he said, "Hey, you need to go see a priest, in the African tradition." At the time I was thinking, "Darn! I can't do nothing right. I tried to kill myself, and *blew that*."

I went to see the priest thinking that, and dragging some of my Catholic stuff behind me, and expected to hear hell-fire and brimstone when the shells hit the table. The man told me, "Love Goddess wants you to know, 'You ain't about to die. Forget it. What has happened to you is just a test to call your attention to the fact that you are marked for the priesthood.' I don't know when, dear-heart, but *one* day you *will* be a priest. She's got some serious work for you to do so you might as well stop shucking and jiving, and commit to doing it. And ain't nothing wrong with you! You ain't crazy. You ain't cursed. You ain't none of that. All you got to do is get on your stick, and do your work." In fact, he said, "You are one who is favored by Her. The best jewels are tempered in the hottest fire, then dipped in the coldest water. Understand it."

Taking on the responsibilities and learnings of the priesthood for me is just another snapshot from the big vision. It's like an opportunity to get the tools that I need to fulfill the work. The work really is what my life is about. I've seen times when I couldn't breathe. I tried to inhale and air wouldn't come in. And then I say, "Ooh – is it time to go home?!" Then I say, "Mommy, I still have work to do." And my breath comes back.

I really don't fully understand it. It seems to me that there are times when my head is empty, my heart is bleeding, my body cannot move, and I go from being a seven-year-old girl to a five-thousand-year-old woman in the run of the day. There are times that I seem to age rapidly in a few moments. And then I am this old, old woman, hundreds of years old. A woman who has seen too much, done too much, and *felt too much*. A woman who cannot stand another moment in this place. And when she shows up, it's more than I can deal with. It's like I void out. I turn something off because there's nothing but this pain. And I don't even know how to describe it because there's nothing but this pain. And I don't even know how to describe it except the physical manifestation of it is I will fall asleep for three days, or I will move across a dance floor, and bust my feet so that I'm on a cane. I just call it being world-weary.

I had a part in a play once, called *Episode from an Ancient Script*. The play scared me because in that play I was what they called "Gleaming, Golden Spider-Woman," who was the "All-Seeing Mother of Time." She had lived for centuries, and for centuries she had tried to warn humans of actions that they were committing which would lead to their own demise. For centuries nobody ever listened to her. So throughout this play I was like this thread that kept saying, "The young man has made friends with this Dutchman who's a slaver, who's trading him beads." And the young man is running off stage, and I would say, "Young man – Beware of ships!"

I *feel* that way sometimes. When I did that part, I said, "Ooh, Teish – there's something . . . why did they pick you for this part?" And I stopped acting for a little while. But I feel that way sometimes. Beware of ships. . . .

It's interesting that my Goddess is a vulture. There's at least two ways to look at it. The vulture doesn't kill anybody. She simply removes the debris, eats it, and passes it through her body, then drops it as compost somewhere. In my tradition, one of the roles of the Vulture Goddess is to pick up the energy of the sacrifice and take it to the Divine. I look at that sometimes, because our Love Goddess, Oshun, has various aspects, and they're associated with various creatures in nature. There's the spider, there's the parrot, there's the peacock. But the aspect of her that is with me is the vulture.

I came up in a community in the South where it was taken for granted that if a woman in our neighbourhood has a baby, the women in the neighborhood were going to clean the house, cook her meals, and look after her children for the next two weeks. That was taken for granted. I grew up in the kind of environment where we made hair grease from prickly pear, cough syrup from white onions. I never had to pose the question to myself, "Will you heal?" The question was, "With what tools?"

I did a lot of touching people through my art which folks told me was healing, through dance and drama. I did a lot of political work which was intended to be healing, and in some ways was.

After that needy winter when I felt myself coming into a kind of power I started doing empathetic healing. Here we go with the vulture again – the illness or the ill condition from which a person is suffering is brought into the healer, and then cast out of her. Therein is the trick and the problem. More and more I am realizing that my dispelling techniques need improving. In fact, I made a decision not to do anymore laying on of hands, and no more mental health work, in terms of people in half-way houses and institutions, or even with people in prison, until I do what we all must do, which is to heal myself.

I have got to heal myself before I can with pride continue to call myself a healer. I can remember recently saying to my Goddess, "Mommy, take me out of the intensive care unit and put me in the well-baby clinic – *please!*" I don't want to be a heavy.

Some people are given gifts like the fella from Brazil, Arego, who can take a rusty knife and plunge it in somebody's body, and pull it out and cancer is gone, and there's no scar. There's a place where I said, "I don't want to be that heavy. Give me some people who just need a *little* bit of exercise, or a little bit of help to move into top form. Take me out of intensive care. I can't handle it."

What I've seen happen since I made that request is, with my responsibilities that have presented themselves to me as a priestess, I now work in the well-baby clinic, and every so often she sends me something from the emergency room, just to say, "Don't forget, kid. There's more to come. Don't get lazy on me."

At this point in time I'm not calling myself a healer. I'm calling myself one who needs to be healed, because I really do feel that way. However, that's not what is reported to me by the people I interact with. The people I interact with say, "Well, regardless of what you say, you're still doing it."

Maybe it's just my perception that's changed. I haven't done massages. I haven't prescribed any herbs. I do however give healing prayers for other people. I do cleansing baths for others, but I am trying not to do the type of empathetic healing any more where the negative energy is taken on by me.

Right now it seems to me that the gift that She has laid on me is the ability – what we call "Good Mouth." I am amazed, being a little country girl from the South, having complexes about accent and lack of education, etc., that I can talk to all kinds of people, and be understood. A lot of that has gone into the writing of my book.

It's been a real interesting feeling, because here, the two of us sitting down, I can look in your eyes, I can see us both break into chills at the same time. There's no question in either of our minds that psychic sympathy is going on here. We're being affected by each other. Ironically, when I sit down to write or when this book sits down to write me, it seems as if every strand of hair on my head is a wire that is connecting to some sister over there. I don't know her name, I can't see her face, but she is over there. I'm plugged into these women. As I write I put some information down on the page. There are even places where I have to say, "Sister, I *hear* you!" I know what your thought is at this time, which is a real trip because nobody's read it yet so who am I talking to? Who am I talking to?

I can sit still and be tired. I can sit right here, and find myself saying, "What is this weight?" Once it becomes clear and takes form, then I know what to do with it, and sometimes it comes into that overload that I just void out. Yes, it can get to be very very heavy to always be so tuned in, but like everything else it's a double-edged sword. I know, I have a certain affinity with my girl friend Bea. I know when Bea is crying even if I haven't heard from her. I know when Vivien is angry, which can be burdensome.

But at the same time I have seen occasions when I had gotten myself into a situation when I was overworked, hadn't eaten, and was too weak to move from the table. Moonstar came running up the stairs, ripping at the door, saying, "What's wrong with you, girl?! Can't you get out of my head. I know there's something wrong with you here." So the rescue comes too. I don't fully understand it, except that there are kindred spirits who are plugged in, the connections are made. The juices flow. I just have to take the batteries out once in a while!

Profile 4

Tsultrim Allione

*Tsultrim Allione is a spiritual teacher, and author of **Woman of Wisdom**. She is a former Buddhist nun who transmits ancient complex body of Tibetan Buddhism. This profile is extracted from **Woman of Wisdom** and lectures by Tsultrim Allione.*

It's always difficult to say when my spiritual walk began, but when I was nineteen I had the opportunity to travel to India and Nepal and proceed with a search which had had few external reference points up until then. My friend and spiritual sister Victress Hitchcock and I traveled to India and stayed with her parents who were in the diplomatic corps in Calcutta, and then we went on to Kathmandu.

One day as we were exploring the upper stories of a house in Kathmandu, we went out on a balcony, and in the distance I saw a small hill at the top of which was a white dome topped by a golden spire. It looked like something from a fairy tale, glittering invitingly in the bright sunlight. We were told that this was called "The Monkey Temple" as it was inhabited by wild monkeys, but its real name was Swayambhu, which means "self-sprung." This small hill topped with a cluster of temples and a huge Tibetan stupa is sacred to both the Nepalese and the Tibetans.

We rose the next day long before dawn and joined the pre-dawn summer fertility procession going down from Kathmandu to Swayambhu. We staggered up hundreds of stone steps amongst ancient stone Buddhas and wild monkeys to the vast round steps. We wandered around the stupa which is like a large, full, white skirt with a gilded spire, amidst the singing, banging Nepalese and the humming Tibetans who were circumabulating the stupa, spinning the prayer wheels which line the lower portion of the round dome. We were just catching our breath when several six-foot-long horns emerged from the adjacent Tibetan monastery and started to make an unbelievable sound. It was a long, deep, whirring, haunting wail that took me out somewhere beyond the highest Himalayan peaks and at the same time back into my mother's womb.

I was so moved by this place that I took a small hut on the neighboring hill, and began to rise very early in the morning, and make the rounds of the Tibetan monasteries on Swayambhu hill as they were chanting their morning rituals and having their first cups of Tibetan tea.

The monastery which attracted me particularly was the one right near the stupa. I used to linger there, sitting in an out-of-the-way corner at the back of the temple. One day I arrived early in the morning as usual and found they had left a little carpet there for me to sit on, and a cup of morning tea. From that day onward the little carpet was always waiting for me, and one of the monks, Gyalwa, who became my friend, always made sure I had tea. It was as if the monks understood my bond with the place and the irresistible pull I felt from the stupa. As I sat there I felt as though part of myself, which had up until then remained empty, was being filled.

A joyful sense of being in the blessings which were almost tangibly present began to steal over me. When I returned to the West I stayed only a year because I experienced an overwhelming nostalgia for the Tibetans. When I returned to Swayambhu in December of 1969, I immediately noticed a hubbub of activity and an incredible assortment of monks, yogis with long matted hair, and Tibetans in an assortment of regional costumes. I learned that this was because His Holiness Karmapa, the head of the Kagyu school lineage, had come to Kathmandu for the first time in thirteen years. He was staying at the same monastery near the stupa which I had visited every morning during my first visit to Nepal. I was a bit put off by all the pomp and pageantry and the pushing Tibetan crowds. Then something unexplainable started to happen to me. I started to feel very agitated and was unable to eat or sleep much. I knew I had to make a connection with someone there. Of course the obvious person was the Karmapa, but perversely I was sure it was someone else. I went around for several days looking for signs, becoming more and more agitated.

Then one day I was reading through the sadhana Trungpa Rinpoche had given me in Scotland on my way back to Nepal. I noticed the continual references to Karmapa. Suddenly it dawned on me that it was obviously an auspicious coincidence that I had arrived at Kathmandu at the same time as his visit and that he was there in "my monastery." At the same time I came across a line in the sadhana which said, "The only offering I can make is to follow your example." Since he was a monk it was suddenly clear to me that I should follow his example and take the robes.

The next morning I went directly to the monastery on Swayambhu, and, disregarding all formalities, walked in, offered him some flowers and indicated that I wanted to cut off my hair. He laughed and then gave me a look I shall never forget. It was as though he was seeing everything: the past, the present, and the future. Then he nodded his head and asked me to sit down. It was decided that I was to be ordained a week later in Bodhgaya, where the Buddha had reached full illumination under the Bodhi tree.

I was given my ordination on the full moon in January 1970 in Bodhgaya, by Karmapa in the presence of the four major tulkus in the Kagyu lineage: Tai Situ, Jamgon Kongtrul, Shamarpa, and Gyaltsab. I was told by the Karmapa's translator that, before I had come to him in Kathmandu, he had seen me in a crowd and had said that I would become a nun and that I had been his disciple in a previous lifetime. At my ordination I was given the name Karma Tsultrim Chodron, which means "the Disciple Torch of Dharma in the Lineage of the Karmapa." I have kept this name because it reminds me of the preciousness of this encounter.

When I returned to Nepal, Gyalwa found me a room next to the stupa which was so small that I could sit in the middle and touch all the walls. Here I cooked, studied, slept and meditated. My lesson started at 6.30 a.m. I was taught by two other nuns who had a rigorous meditation schedule and had only this time to teach me. My room was like a little tree-house. The windows opened into some huge old trees. Living so near the stupa I came to know its life, day and night, and through the seasons. What happened around the stupa was a condensation of the magical religious life and festivals of both the Nepalese and the Tibetans.

My favorite thing to study was the biographies of the great teachers of Tibetan Buddhism. Since I was trying to follow the same path, I found the stories of their struggles and the ensuing realizations that they gained tremendously helpful and inspiring. I found tidbits of stories of women here and there, but there was nothing very substantial. Now it is obvious to me why I longed for the stories of women, but then, amazingly, I did not consciously wonder about the lack of women's biographies. It was part of my conditioning to accept that all the important yogis were men, but I think that unconsciously the roots of the research for *Women of Wisdom* began at that time.

After two and a half years in India I decided to return to the United States to see my family. I found that being a nun there became more of a hindrance than a blessing. I continued to wear the robes for another year and then, for reasons which I go into in my book, I gave up my nun vows and shortly after married. Within a year I went from being a solitary nun to being a mother. My first pregnancy was followed nine months later by another.

When I was in my second pregnancy, a group of women where I lived in Washington State decided to meet and discuss their babies and breastfeeding problems. After one meeting we decided we did not want to talk about our babies, but we wanted to explore our interior lives, and to hear each others' stories. These meetings were a revelation in many ways. I began to be fascinated by the female experience and to cherish the company of women. In India, being a woman had been something I had hoped would not get in the way. Through this group I realized that being a woman was not a liability, but rather that women had, amongst other qualities, an ability to heal, to have direct insight into situations, and to give support without judging. I began to love being a woman, being with women, and wanted to understand women's unique experiences more deeply. I then realized the Tibetan Buddhist women's stories had not been told. I longed to join my spiritual path with my awareness of myself as a woman and began to think about researching the lives of Tibetan yoginis.

When I was on a group retreat in California in 1981, given by Namkai Norbu Rinpoche, one night we were doing the Chod practice. At a certain point we were invoking the presence of Machig Lapdron, visualizing her as a youthful, white dakini. Suddenly a wild-looking old woman appeared very close to me. She had grey hair streaming from her head, and she was naked, with dark golden-brown skin. Her breasts hung pendulously and she was dancing. She was coming out of a dark cemetery. The most impressive thing about her was the look in her eyes. They were very bright, and the expression was one of challenging invitation mixed with mischievous joy, uncompromising strength and compassion. She was inviting me to join her dance.

Afterwards I realized that this was a form of Machig Lapdron. She was a woman who really embodied the wisdom of the feminine. She had fed babies with those breasts yet she was undomesticated. She was fearless yet compassionate, ecstatic yet grounded, and above all she was inviting me with her confidence and her joy.

That same week I began having repetitive dreams that I must go back to Swayambhu. In each dream there were different kinds of obstacles to get to the mountain and every morning I woke up with an incredible urgent desire to get there.

When I did finally arrive in March of 1982, I was given the biography of Machig Lapdron in the monastery next to the stupa. That was the first of six stories which became *Women of Wisdom*.

In my research for the book I read about the matriarchal culture in pre-Aryan India, 3000–1500 BC. The culture and religion was oriented around the Goddess as the dynamic force in the universe. In these Tantric teachings was a sense of integration of spirituality into life, and life in itself was perceived as sacred. There was not the typical patriarchal split between spirit and nature. This culture was largely destroyed by invasions of lighter skinned Aryans who were patriarchal

tribes from the north. The Aryans slowly took over the native
people and established the caste system. The word caste means
color, so the caste system was a hierarchical society divided by
color. The white male Brahmin priests were on the top of the
ladder, and the darker skinned native people were on the
bottom.

The native peoples were the holders of a lineage of teachings
which became a system of religious practices of the conquered
matriarchal culture. The sacred practices evoked, developed,
and celebrated the innate energy, the innate spirituality within.
There was no separation of body and spirit.

In the sixth century AD there was a re-emergence of two
bodies of writings, the Tantras and the Puranas (ancient
teachings), which had powerful Goddess imagery which had
survived from ancient times. It was from these teachings and
from Buddhism that the Tibetans learned.

In ancient Tantra the body was trained in yoga so that it
became the central mandala. There are ways that we think of as
ways of becoming more spiritual, such as by being a
vegetarian, by being more and more refined, and by living in
pure places. These were not the ways of the tantrikas. That is
not how they lived. They lived inviting the so-called impure
aspects of life by living in the cemeteries, engaging in sexual
practices, eating meat, and consuming intoxicants.

Tantra and Tantric practices continue to this day. In Tibetan
Tantra the feminine energy is the dynamic wisdom and the
masculine is skillful action. The dakini, who is feminine, is an
integral part of Tantric practices. Because wrathful and peaceful
deities are used in visualization practices, the Tantric practitioner
has a vast range of energies to tap, a wide variety of archetypes,
if you will. The fact that the feminine in Tantra may be
displayed as a wrathful, naked, dancing figure completely
opens up the one-dimensional Madonna image, which is all our
culture has given us to identify with. The female body in
ancient religions was in itself considered to be magical, sacred
and inspiring. It was not until women themselves were
considered profane that the female body was also shameful.

The most important aspect of the feminine in Tantra is the
dakini. Being a dynamic principle, the dakini is energy itself; a

positive contact with her brings about a sense of freshness and
magic, though she can also be tricky. Ideally by activating this
energy she becomes an agent for unfolding awareness for both
men and women, but this energy can turn suddenly and pull
the rug out from under you if you get too attached and fixated.
She acts as a spiritual midwife, helping the Tantric practitioner
to give birth to wisdom. She may appear as a human being, as
a goddess – either peaceful or wrathful – or she may be
perceived as the general play of energy in the phenomenal
world.

There are stories of Tibetan or Indian yogis like Tilopa or
Naropa – going to low caste women for teaching which
included sexual practices. It isn't that these were the only
women available for their sexual practices. It was because these
were the women who held the ancient pre-Aryan teachings.

The reason why the lines of women teachers did not flourish
in Tibetan Buddhism is because of the ambiguous status of
women in Tibet. They believe that being born a woman shows
a lower state of development. On the other hand one of the
vows a practitioner of Tibetan Tantra takes is to not disparage
women and to see them as the incarnation of wisdom. These
are people who are doing practices which have to do with
working with feminine deities. What I found out in my
research is that in Tibet there's a combination of matriarchal
and patriarchal traditions. This creates an ambiguous status for
women and so they generally remain in the background, with a
few exceptions.

I think that yogis in patriarchal Hindu and Buddhist societies
were experiencing a lot of what we are experiencing in our
present society, that is the need for feminine wisdom, because
then, as now, the masculine was taken to the nth degree.

The yogi Naropa was very caught up in Buddhist philosophy
and logic. He was very disconnected from his intuition, and
from his feminine side. On one day he was sitting outside
reading a Buddhist book of logic. A shadow fell across his
book. He turned around, and saw an incredibly ugly woman.
She asked him if he understood the *words* or the *meaning* of
what he was reading. He said, "I understand *both*." She got
furious, and said, "You don't! You only understand the

words!" That punctured his balloon. His only way of coping
with it was to analyze her thirty-two ugly features with
Buddhist logic, but afterwards he left the monastery, gave up
his monk's vows, and began the search for his guru Tilopa.

It took Naropa twelve years to get through his conceptuality
and preconceptions. He went through incredible suffering as a
result of taking everything literally, and being stuck in his
conceptual teaching. His guru once said to him, when they
were standing at the top of a pagoda, "If I had a disciple, he
would jump off this temple." Naropa took it very literally and,
to demonstrate his commitment, he jumped off the building,
and landed as a mess below. His teacher came to him and said,
"You don't understand anything. Get up and try again."

There's another great story that's in my book *Women of
Wisdom*. It's about the man who was living in retreat, with a
woman who was his teacher and companion. He went into
samadhi for twelve years. But before he went into samadhi
he asked the woman to make him radish curry. Then when he
came out of samadhi, after twelve years, he said to her,
"Where's my radish curry?" She couldn't believe it! She said to
him. "You've been in samadhi for twelve years, and the first
thing you ask for is *radish curry*?! It isn't even the season for
radishes."

He said, "Well, if you won't make me radish curry, then I'm
going to the mountains to meditate." She said, "Well, you can
go to the mountains and meditate as long as you want. There
are a lot of animals that live in the caves in the mountains, but
that doesn't mean you are going to get enlightened any more
than they are. Unless you free yourself from attachment, and
unless your meditation is having some kind of effect on your
life, you can go wherever you want and meditate, but it's not
going to make any difference. He thought about it, and decided
to stay with her. She had something to teach him.

You see those stories again and again. What's really
happening is that these women are teaching. They may not sit
on a throne, or wear special clothes. They teach in the living
situation. The dakinis come in many forms, and they often
transmit teachings through energy. The reason why they were
often sexual partners with whomever they were teaching, and

were not puritanical in the sense that they might change partners every year or every six years, is that sexual practice is an integral part of Tantra. Also, Tantra is outside conventional control structures. It wasn't promiscuousness. Sexuality was actually part of the path, something sacred, a method for realization.

There is another story of a monk who was sitting doing his meditation on Vajrayogini. He was intent on his meditation, and his shrine was arranged very neatly. Suddenly a woman came in the room dragging a piece of bloody meat. She said, "Eat this!" and shoved the meat at him. He said, "How dare you! I'm a pure monk!" She was an affront to everything he was doing. She disappeared. The monk went to his guru and told him what had happened. The guru told him that he had failed to recognize Vajrayogini. The real meaning of this may be that he was way out in left field in his understanding of Tantra, which is very earthy. Therefore this confrontation was seen as an interruption.

When I had my first child, the blood, and the earthiness of it was incredibly powerful. Menstrual blood reminds women of their connection to the earth, to the moon, and to nature. In Tantra the menstrual blood is considered sacred and powerful. Many of the Goddesses in pre-Aryan times were red. In Nepal and India they sprinkle red powder on the third eye of the deities. Sometimes it is mixed into a paste with rice. In India women wear red in their parts and third eye. This has to do with the blood of life, the primal matrix which becomes babies, and becomes milk – woman's transformation mysteries, giving form to formless energy. When yogic practitioners taste the mixture of semen and blood, as it hits the throat chakra, that is the secret initiation. A Tantric consort was considered potent during her moon cycle.

In religions in which there is a question of whether or not women have a soul or whether they can attain enlightenment, women are admitted begrudgingly and with many stipulations as to what extent they can participate. When there is an image of a female it tends to be very limited, like the Madonna adoring her male offspring. The aspect of the feminine that is considered to be all right for women is one that portrays us as

being bad, victimized and compassionate. Compassion is
something that is often manifested in women, but it's not the
only transcendent feminine quality. The feminine can also be
powerful, wrathful, sexual, ecstatic, and wild.

What's fantastic about Tantra is that all those aspects are
demonstrated. Women and men practicing Tantra can identify
with the various aspects. There are peaceful manifestations like
Ekajah; semi-wrathful blissful dakinis like Vajrayogini. The
masculine is also multi-dimensional in Tantra, so that male
energy is not put into a one-dimensional role either. There is a
peaceful kind of male, who is very compassionate, like
Chenresi, and there is the wrathful, passionate kind of energy
of the Herukas, and the Mahakalas. In ancient Tantric images,
and especially in Hindu Tantra, the feminine is creative, and
the masculine is receptive. Sexuality has to do with a meshing
of energy. We all have electro-magnetic currents running
through us, and in Tantra these are balanced and developed.
Women and men alternate visualization of male and female
deities.

The Dzog Chen (Maha Ati) teachings, the most ancient
school of meditation in Tibet, also held the feminine in high
esteem. In Dzog Chen traditions, dakinis, the female spiritual
forces, are an absolute integral part of the teachings. The
teachings are often originally written in the mysterious cipher
called the language of the dakini, "the twilight language."
These teachings are transmitted, concealed, and protected by
dakinis. In both Tantra and Dzog Chen the practitioner must
always maintain a positive relationship to the feminine or the
development of the practice will be blocked.

It is fascinating to see that the Dzog Chen tradition shows
many of the political tendencies which were present in
matriarchal societies. Dzog Chen communities tend to be non-
hierarchical, based on cooperation rather than competition,
with communities of families, or loosely formed collections of
hermits of both sexes who have no particular "organizations."
In this situation women practitioners were independent and
flourished.

The Dzog Chen teachings work directly with the energy of
the body, speech, and mind. It is a path of self-liberation rather

than a path of transformation like Tantra. The idea is that we are primordially awake all the time but we have become separated from that state and have forgotten it. In order to return to living from that place of non-duality, one must have first the understanding of what happened, and then through practices, many based on the use of sound, the barriers to remaining in the primordial state are removed. One is not reaching a previously non-existent state, but getting confusion out of the way to see what is under it, like the sun coming out from behind the clouds. Passions are experienced "as they come up" without transformation, like snow falling into the water. Teachers of Dzog Chen in the past have mentioned that women are particularly adapted for these practices as they have an innate capacity to work with energy.

In Tantra, the human body is seen as one of the primary mandalas or the primary transformation base that we have. In Tantra you enter more into your body, and use and train it rather than try to cut yourself off from it, thinking of it as repulsive or as a manifestation of impurity. Sex itself is seen as a means of transformation rather that something that needs to be renounced to reach liberation.

In Tantra the sexual energy is used for the unification of the senses, and the sense objects. When one is practicing Tantra there's the *gan puja*, or feast offering ceremony, in which meat and red wine are consumed. The idea is that while eating and drinking, one enters a state of equanimity, of non-judgment, called "one-taste." What that really means is not that everything tastes the same, but that the original sensation of taste *itself* is entered into and continued in experience. What we usually do is we taste something, and we immediately begin a discursive thought pattern inside ourselves about whatever it is we are eating. This is good, or this is bad, or bitter, or sweet. We pigeon-hole all of our experience instead of remaining in the sensation. If you are in a state of unification with whatever you are eating, then there's a tremendous amount of taste – more taste than we usually have, because we're so caught up in the function of the mind, that we often don't taste our food.

It is the same with the other senses. For example, if you remain in a state of pure presence, just seeing the beautiful sunset, what is seen keeps entering, and entering, and entering. There isn't that point of reflection where you start seeing the sunset and think, "Oh – it's beautiful," or, "Oh – I want to take a picture of it." It's just a continual state of unification.

The reason for sexual imagery is that with sexual contact all the senses are operating. You experience touch, and taste, and smell, and sight, and everything all at once. If you can remain in that state of pure sensation without a discursive division of pleasure as opposed to pain, it becomes very powerful and blissful, because there aren't the resistances or complications that we usually have.

There are some practices which can help to train you in this which are really very simple, everyday situations. When you are exposed to the elements – wind, water, fire, or earth – you can practice integrating with those elements rather than resisting them, in the same way as with the senses practice. If the wind is blowing, let it just blow as if there is no separation between yourself and the wind. When those practices are entered into completely, then you have the manifestation of siddhis. It is possible to go into fire like Padmasambhava and Mandarava, who were burned on a pyre because of their sexual relationship. Because they were able to integrate with the fire, after seven days they were still there in a blissful state. The same principle is there for those who have the ability to walk through walls. When there isn't that sense of reflection and separation, many things are possible. It's not just something theoretical.

Another reason why the Buddhist monks were attracted to the Tantric teachings is because they really work, something really happens. That is also why these traditions did not die out. These traditions are incredibly old. As far as I know they are some of the oldest living traditions which come down to us. It is a source which is still alive, and can still be practiced with experienced guides. It's not something that we have to dig up out of the past and reinvent.

Another spiritual practice that you can do is you can work with the sky. You can lie down, or sit, and fix your gaze on the open sky, not looking toward the sun. Just look at the sky, and let the sky integrate with you, or you with the sky – at that point there's no difference. It's called "namkai – arte" in Tibetan, which means mixing mind with sky. It's an incredibly powerful and wonderful practice. It's also very good if you are at a point in your spiritual practice where you can't stand sitting anymore. If you look at your meditation cushion and want to slam the door and go out for a walk, this is a practice that is a very relaxing and very spacious experience. These practices are the kinds of things that can be done with no particular special props. It's helpful to have certain times to practice these meditations, but never force yourself to do more than you really feel like doing. This has to do with trusting yourself, rather than feeling that you are an enemy that has to be overcome with discipline. You can trust your innate spirituality. You can treat yourself as a spiritual ally, knowing that realization is going to come about if you just give it the space to.

There is also the practice called the "vajra breath" which you can do as you walk, or when you are just sitting at a stoplight in your car, or on a bus. As you inhale you visualize white light coming into you, and mentally say "OM." Hold the breath a bit and visualize a red light and sound "HUM." This is a very simple and powerful practice. If you keep doing it for a while you will find yourself entering into a different state of mind.

Tantric practices need to be transmitted by teachers who have received the transmissions. The initiations and the teachers are available. The Dzog Chen teachings of integration that I've talked about are not Tantric teachings. Dzog Chen is another tradition that is put into this big bundle that's called Tibetan Buddhism. According to my teacher, these teachings come from around Mount Kailash, in a place called Shang-Shung. They are teachings of self-liberation, or of things liberating themselves. You work directly with with something like the elements, and rather than visualizing a deity, or chanting a mantra, you work with the elements themselves. When you work with sound, you work with the dimension of entering into sound, rather than mantra where you are using the energy of sound for transformation. Dzog Chen teachings are a tremendous resource. The person who first taught the

Dzog Chen teachings on the earth was Garab Dorje. They were taught in thirteen solar systems before they were taught on the earth.

Garab Dorje said that more women than men would attain the rainbow body which is the result or goal of Dzog Chen teachings. The rainbow body is the dissolution of the physical body into light at the time of death. The reason for this, he explained, was that these practices work with energy, and women have a natural capacity to work with energy. The body is naturally light anyway, so with the dissolution of energy all the elements return to their natural state which is light. These teachings have been practiced since before Christ, and since then many people have achieved the rainbow body at death. It isn't something that just happened 2,000 years ago. It is still happening in the twentieth century. This was something that shocked the Chinese when they invaded Tibet. They came to kill the "corrupt yogis" and instead they found piles of hair and fingernails, but no bodies!

One of the things I'm doing now is researching places connected to feminine energy, like the sacred caves. Caves are the womb transformation places of the earth, in the same way that a woman's womb is the transformation place of the human race. Caves are like the wombs of the earth. In ancient times people would go into caves for self-transformation. I started doing research on these caves and then found that it was hard to find them. I also found that there are sacred springs, mountains, temples, groves, etc. So I decided to do a guide book to feminine power places. With this book one would be able to find these places all over the world. If you wanted to make a pilgrimage to some of these places, you'd know where they are.

It's not just that this is an entertaining thing to do, but it's part of healing the earth. To go to the places of the Goddess, and to places where the earth has been revered in the form of the Goddess, will help to heal the earth, because the earth feels our thoughts. These places are like our ears, our nose, or our mouth. If we go there and make offerings, and we give our Mother Earth our healing energy, then she will be helped in her healing. We can be politically active, and I think that we need to do that, but also by doing this kind of thing we can affect real planetary change. I think that the earth is a sentient being. She feels and reacts. If we can communicate our concern, and our sense of the sacred through these power places, which are like acupuncture points, or sense organs, then it can help the earth's whole healing process, and it can obviously help us as well.

Profile 5

Rowena Pattee

*Rowena Pattee is a visionary visual artist and the author of **Song to Thee: Divine Androgyne** and **Moving with Change: A Woman's Reintegration of the I Ching**. She has made five films, the latest being **Tree of Life** and **Passages**, which are "cosmic animation." She was also the cinematographer for the Findhorn documentary which has been shown widely on TV and in the theaters. Her work has been exhibited widely, is included in collections in over forty states and is in the permanent collection of the National Gallery of Israel. She is on the faculty of John F. Kennedy University and the California Institute of Integral Studies where she teaches I Ching, Key World Myths and Symbols, Sacred Art, and Shamanic Art and Ritual Healing. She has recently been appointed to the Rudolph Schaffer chair of Art and Creativity Studies at CIIS.*

Living from the "sun in the heart" is the main experience in my shamanic "work." There is really no point at which this "work" begins or ends. It is a continuous awakening to divinity in each moment, walking in forests, being with others, organizing programs, planting seeds, driving, skiing, drinking tea and resting.

Gradually throughout my life I've come to a more voluntary and conscious dilation of my whole being. This opening has enabled many spontaneous, wonderful things to happen to me. This is not to say there is no effort involved. One must make an effort to enable the effortless to happen.

Meditation since 1963 when I met Zen master Shunryu Suzuki Roshi has been my main effort. This is an effort to "just be." It involves simple practices like giving attention to posture and breath and mind. I learned through quiet "sitting"

57

regularly everyday, moment by moment, to bring all my disparate desires into one big desire: insight into the truth of whatever's happening and a loving acceptance. You can imagine my gratitude at meeting Shunryu Suzuki Roshi! This occurred when I was painting with sumi ink in the great Chinese-Japanese monochrome tradition of landscape painting. I painted from a remembrance of previous lives in China. Meeting Suzuki Roshi was a recognition. When we first met we just giggled mirthfully for several hours. I wasn't looking for a Zen master. It just happened.

Suzuki Roshi was a great spiritual nourishment so I sought to learn of what he had to teach. I followed him around for a couple of months, but he would not teach me zazen (sitting meditation). Finally he did teach me, and he told me later that he hesitated teaching it to me because I was already a "natural" and he didn't want to change it. But fate introduced me to a few problems which caused reactions throwing me at a "tilt," so that I was "eligible" to learn this simple but profound practice.

Through Zen practice and the presence of Suzuki Roshi I was brought into a singularity which combines being brilliant, nothing and all-encompassing of sentient beings. Through the "sun in the heart" and disciplined attention I found a compassionate embrace and a sword of truth in the midst of life. This is an on-going process.

Now shamanic "work" has come to me spontaneously also. I made many shamanic drawings, prints and paintings in the 1960s and wrote stories based on shamanic experiences from Siberian, Amerindian, and Australian sources, but only since 1984 have I clearly been "called." Again I was not seeking it. My interpretation is that divine beings, spirits and those with "master plans" for the regeneration of humanity appear in visions, voices and direct cognition to anyone who is dilated enough to receive their directives. Such persons are needed now.

Doubters may call such visions hallucinations, but there is a criterion for true visionary directives as distinct from delusory psychic content: the integrity of the person and whether they nourish the environment and people around them. It may take a while to manifest the spirit directives, but their authenticity is known by the beneficent quality the person receiving them has on humanity and the environment.

This often takes sacrifice in the same way that mothering takes sacrifice. Women shamans are returning because the feminine qualities of intuition, nurturing, compassion and the power to bear and manifest are needed for the forthcoming culture. I am not an extreme feminist, but all my life have sought only balance and complementarity in matters of the masculine and feminine, both literally and symbolically. Both of my published books, *Song to Thee: Divine Androgyne* and *Moving with Change: A Women's Reintegration of the I Ching*, deal with the complementarity of male and female. In my own life, because of the "sun in the heart" I have been graced with the courage to allow both my masculine and feminine sides to grow and come into a creativity.

Part of my shamanic preparation has been testing my Zen practice by transforming the abandoned ruin of the Avery Brundage Estate in Santa Barbara, into a temple, home and studio. It is called the "Cave-of-Dawning." This developed my masculine side, but was based on feminine intuition. I received intuitive directives to do this. It was seemingly impractical and irrational! I didn't even have enough money to buy the lot, let alone renovate this 120-foot ruin! Yet because I was receptive I was able to become active and do the unpredictable and seemingly impossible. Following intuition is living with the "heart-sun."

I feel contemporary shamans must deal with all the realms of life, including money, resources as well as spirit. In this building project my meager monetary resources were seemingly insufficient and my income unreliable, as an artist. No banker in his right mind would advise me to undertake this task. But spirit directives have an intrinsic nourishment. You just *know* it's right. As a result, I have found that actions taken from intuition become more practical and stable because they are based on true directives rather than greed or defensiveness. At the time I had no intention of selling the "Cave-of-Dawning," but just as I was spiritually directed to do it, I was similarly directed to release and leave it. The work of completion took two years and then I had four years of creating the *Tree of Life* animated film. We also had many group celebrations of the arts and sciences at the Cave-of-Dawning. When I sold it, I quintupled my money, but I originally thought I would live there the rest of my life.

Such work developed my masculine side in taking action, and I learned all manner of architectural, plumbing, electrical, masonry and carpentry skills. I believe the greatest shamans have always known how to function on all levels. This preparation was primarily a part of purification and tests as initiations.

My Zen training stood me in good stead on many fronts. During this architectural project I also had fearful neighbours who thought my method of construction in this ruin might lower the property values! Not reacting to these neighbour's fears enabled the "law of the boomerang" to work: they lost all four county hearings unanimously and then put up their house for sale and moved. This was a shamanic exorcism. I was operating under a pillar of white light directing my life. I wished these neighbours well, but I had no room for nonsense. All I did was work, pray and sleep and work again. Because I could have lost the whole property, these neighbours unwittingly enabled me to come into a higher state of detachment while working very hard. The exorcism purified both the property and myself.

After digging trenches and working in this ruin for five months with a few wonderful unskilled "fellows" (who became very skilled), I went for a ten-day meditation in the forest. During this meditation I received the most clear vision of three Taoist Immortals who gave me a diamond staff and directed me to "learn the language of nature and spirit." This was in September of 1976. In this vision I saw the earth in the future. I saw great suffering but the Immortals told me, "*After a period of travail there will be children who understand the language of nature and spirit.*" I felt an elixir drop from the roof of my mouth and pervade my whole body and then I went into celestial landscapes. I saw an illuminated, crystalline, gem-like earth and drank green tea with an old hermit who greeted me like an old friend! The whole vision is long, but the essence of it is that I was immovable for a long time and I saw and heard things that are mandates for my whole destiny. I was vastly nourished and felt bathed in a subtle elixir for many days.

When I returned to the physical work of the ruin, the exorcism was complete and I glowed. The next year and a half's work was relatively effortless and the place became a nurturing environment for many people. We had wonderful celebrations wherein some of the neighbours who previously signed a petition to have the Cave-of-Dawning torn down were dancing labyrinthian dances, holding hands with hippy types! Fountains, flowers, octagonal pathways, one-hundred-foot mosaic murals were all part of the happy magic. Musicians and dancers came.

I made a dozen mosaic murals based on inner visions, after having studied world myths and symbols for eight years. This is a shamanic art in the sense that it springs from direct visions and inspiration and is a synthesis of symbolic patterns, establishing a cosmology, a mythology, an integral set of symbols whereby one has a point of reference "between the worlds" of spirit and nature. My doctoral thesis is on an integrated "orientation" to world myths and patterns of consciousness for people today. Spirit is generally invisible to the ordinary senses, but is visible to shaman-visionaries. Nature is visible to the ordinary senses and is itself a language of patterns which reveals its spiritual source. Shamans mediate spirit and nature by being fully human.

The ancient Chinese made clear the idea in the triplicity: "Heaven, Human, Earth." This basic shamanic "triple world" scheme is behind every culture that's ever endured: Egypt, India, Sumeria, Amerindia, Persia, Israel. This triplicity is reflected in the Hindu *Sat*, *Chit*, *Ananda* ("being, consciousness, bliss"). "Being" is our ontological source, "consciousness" is the mediator of human beings and nature which, when in alignment with "being," brings bliss, happiness, the shamanic ecstacy. This is not just a theory but is a living reality when you live with a "sun in the heart." Happiness naturally results when the "triple worlds" are connected by human mediators, by shamans.

True giving enables full openness whereby the nourishment

of happiness is received. Here again is the feminine, receptive side. It is received spontaneously and fully when one has given whole-heartedly of one's life. I find myself happier and happier as I get older. I am simply freer of conditions. This entails conscious, voluntary sacrifices. Sacrifice comes from the words "to make sacred." My shamanic life is a whole life of making sacred, seeing everything as sacred.

Of course there is a lot of "janitor work" along the way, lots of garbage to transmute, to create good compost for our seeds of destiny to grow in. Even the garbage is sacred! You just have to know what to do with it. The whole planet is undergoing a "garbage" or "dissolution" phase. It is called *putrefactio* in alchemy. Breakdown of traditions, decomposition, illness, nervous stress, air-noise-water-food pollutions, revolutions, economic precariousness, psychopathologies, excessive military armaments are all part of it. The contemporary shaman includes the ills of the whole planet in her/his domain but does not feel weighed down by it. Lightness and profundity go together when one lives whole-heartedly with spirit directives. But it takes continuous practice of non-reaction to conditions and taking action from a center aligned with the "triple worlds."

My concern is for the earth as a living being and for the regeneration of humanity at its roots. Its roots are spiritual and that's why shamans, and especially balanced, clear women shamans, are needed today. Shamans directly "tune in" to spiritual directives and have integrated their lives so that these directives can be manifested in daily life on earth. This is a true death and regeneration experience.

All my life I have undergone some degree of death and regeneration. I went through a complete experience of death in the "void," *shunyata*, in the late 1960s during an intensive seven-day "session" while in Suzuki Roshi's presence. In my own experience death and regeneration have been intensified in recent years. I have felt my whole body undergo a radical vibrational change and have seen iridescent beings decompose and recompose my body. I have received many etheric, brilliantly energized gem implantations in my new body. This sounds preposterous to people who have not experienced these things.

The current "dissolution/putrefaction" phase of civilisation is the necessary death and release before regeneration and reculturation is possible. The heart of the shamanic experience is creativity coming out of a clash and fusion of opposites.

One reason I feel I have been "called" to shamanic "work" is that I have never stopped drawing and painting since I was a child. This has kept me true to "what is." Creativity keeps you clear and keeps the channels open *between* worlds.

In the past year or so I've been directed by spirits to make shamanic robes. There are eight in all and each has a specific function and quality, all of which are part of a cosmology created from the patterns of my own unique destiny, linked with world myths and archetypes. The robes are different ways to express the art of my own life. Whenever I resisted making these robes I felt ill. Responding to the directives I felt immense power. Often the spirits would tell me to fast or only eat green apples while making the robes! Many synchronous things happened during their process, especially with regard to birds and the weather. More details on this are written in an article "Six Shamanic Robes" delivered at the second Shamanic International Conference in California and published in the proceedings of that conference, edited by Ruth Inge-Heinze. The names of the robes in the order that they were given to me are: "White Eagle" (September 1984), "Heart of Heaven and Earth" (December 1984), "Happy Death Hawk" (January 1985), "Black Buffalo" (February-April 1985), "Blue Woman" (March-November 1985), "White Buffalo" (March-December 1985), "White Egret Essence" (April-December 1985) and "Diamond Fool" (future). I've been shown that these robes have a function in the future for rituals at sacred centers which are part of the plan for the regeneration of humanity.

Since 1983 I have used the drum both for my own spirit "journeys" and others'. The drum is a direct way for spirit as "being" to enter "consciousness" and through a process of clearing to arrive at "ecstatic vision." I experience different qualities of subtle energy while beating the drum in different places around the perimeter or center of the drum. Colors, gems and emanations in direct correspondence with the sound came from this process as a rich qualitative universe.

I voluntarily and consciously can go into visionary states of consciousness where I meet with spirit beings and traverse many realms. It is important that one keeps the "sun in the heart" to keep the highest truth uppermost and not get lost along the way. Shamanic work is not something to dally with.

One time while "journeying" I found myself in a desert in the south-western part of the US with herds and herds of dark buffalo. I was one among the buffalo, running across the desert. At a certain point we went down into the earth in a zig-zag fashion on diagonal ramps, deep down into the earth. There deep in the earth I saw blood and gore, hunks of flesh. The "buffalo people" told me this was their sacrifice to the people. They asked, "Will you be with us?" There was no hesitation since this is what was true at the moment. I then ascended alone from the depths of the earth while the dark buffalo people remained below. At the point of emergence there was "White Buffalo" with blue twinkling eyes. (White Buffalo is one of my main spirit guides, whom I encountered first while conducting a shamanic workshop. "He" appeared at the moment my 95–year-old mystic friend Shunyata (named by Ramana Maharshi) was hit by a car and later died. The blue twinkling eyes in the "White Buffalo" were Shunyata's eyes!)

Now "White Buffalo" was standing in the desert and immediately I got on his back and we were off across the country to the north. I was shown sacred centers all up the north-west coast, Alaska, across the Bering Straight, Manchuria, China, Indonesia, Australia, New Zealand, the Pacific Islands and back through Chile, Peru, Middle America and up the coast of California to the south-western desert. Then I saw the desert burst into bloom, fountains rise up and the land become green.

Since that time I have seen in "journeys" more aspects of the sacred centers, a certain number of which are underground. I have seen deeply into aspects of the structure of the earth and have been given directives to create "crystal earth cards" which will attune people's consciousness with spirit and the earth. A stronger, more wholesome connection between the "triple worlds" is essential for healing humanity and the earth.

In vision I have gone into the Pacific Ocean many times where I have eight "dolphin guides" who take me right down to a special place at the bottom where a great vortex of energy is. The sea creatures are suffering from the result of human malaise and ever seek nourishment from the center of this vortex. At the center of the vortex is a lapis lazuli trapdoor! By the power of the "eight dolphins" I moved the trapdoor just a fraction and saw into a realm of vast iridescent energy which can heal all ills. I felt my whole body cleansed and energized.

I was then shown a large translucent obelisk which has its base at the lapis lazuli trapdoor and rises up through the Pacific out into the sky. I saw the underground sacred centers as points of illumination round the Pacific Basin with laser-beam-like rays focused at the top of the obelisk, creating a great star. *I knew that this is the axis of the New World and that this "needle of light" could emanate infinite healing energy to the whole earth.* It is clear that for this to occur there needs to be true, integral, visionary human beings who can focus spiritual energy into the underground sacred centers all around the Pacific Basin. A network of loving human beings totally dedicated to truth is necessary.

I am shown only glimpses of a "master plan" which I know can heal and make whole. In addition to spirits who appear in animal forms, I regularly meet with "Blue Pharaoh," "Eagle Crooked Path," "Arhat" and "White Egret Woman."

The Blue Pharaoh has shown me how to pass through crystal cities, out through the molecular, atomic and subatomic harmonies into an electric, azure-blue limitless realm of infinite purity. The Blue Pharaoh's realm is sapphire and blue topaz.

My Indian guide is called Eagle Crooked Path and he is a very ancient being. Though he has an outrageous sense of humor he never laughs. He is compassionate above all, but appears stern. His realm is emerald and the ruby of the heart.

The Arhat shows me the truth of realms far beyond all the other visionary realms. I first saw him after Shunyata died and I asked where my friend had gone. I was then taken by White

Buffalo to a certain firmament and then I was left to ascend by myself. In a luminous darkness I saw two meditating beings sitting on two large golden Bodhi leaves. They came together and merged and transported me up to the Arhat. I felt such humility, gratitude and purification at once in the presence of this being that nothing can express it. The Arhat teaches by pure presence. Only once has he spoken to me.

The Arhat is my highest guide and master and his realm is jade. He teaches me many things about the rare subtle point and singularity of truth. I feel a strong connection with Suzuki Roshi through him.

Behind the Arhat is a crystalline cave and a tiger (who sometimes appears as a black panther). On subsequent "journeys" I have ridden the tiger and gone through the cave. At the other end of the cave I can see the "current world situation" as patterns down an abyss. This is not literal, but a sense of the quality of the contemporary sense. Since I rarely read the newspapers, this is a way to catch up on the "news"!

White Egret Woman has appeared most recently in visions. She is a being clothed in white iridescent robes of the finest essences. It is the same kind of energy as I experience on the other side of the lapis lazuli trapdoor at the bottom of the Pacific Ocean. She directly brings happiness and joy. I see her in underground sacred centres and many places in hidden chambers in the crystalline earth. Her realm is lapis lazuli and diamond.

For the past few years I have been blessed with repeated experiences of vast heart openings to infinity where I am fully enveloped in iridescent light. This is "diamond–heart–energy" where the "sun in the heart" has become stable and incorruptible. After these experiences I literally cannot see anything but light for half an hour, even if I want to see with ordinary senses! At first this troubled me, thinking I might be going blind, but I have learned over and over to release any fear and anxiety.

In addition to these guides and others, I meet with a Council of Elders. They give me counsel when critical issues come up. For a while I was living excessively in vision and had difficulty "grounding." The Council of Elders said to me, "Run barefoot on white mountains." Last summer I ran barefoot on the white granite at Yosemite in the Sierras and this balanced me. You see, they even take care of our physical being!

People sometimes come to me for healing. I make no claims to being a healer, but a few people have become more integral and centered and happy around me. My way is teaching by whole-hearted living and I know I will help establish holistic schools.

I know that a whole creative reculturation process is coming which will build a New World. I can see it and anything I can see in the subtle planes *can* become manifest in the physical. First is the alignment with divine directives, then the breakdown and dissolution of old values, then the clean-up and purification. Then comes the dilation to receive more spiritual directives, the extraction out of past repositories, the essences of what we can creatively go on with (in religions, myth, symbols, science, values). Then comes the build-up and regeneration on a truly global scale. True creativity will flow.

We have lived like caterpillars, producing and consuming long enough. Now, as a civilization, we are entering the disorientation experience inside the chrysalis. The DNA which can create a beautiful butterfly is in spiritual directives. We need only to learn to be receptive, integral and true. Then a brilliant holistic culture will be born out of the "pea soup" disorientation that is necessary in the present chrysalis phase. The way is to be yourself fully and trust active peace.

Profile 6

Ruth-Inge Heinze

Ruth-Inge Heinze (PhD, University of California, Berkeley) has been working in the fields of psychological anthropology and comparative religion for the last twenty-six years. She taught and conducted research in Europe, North America, and Asia, specializing in religious practices, alternate states of consciousness, and healing. She has published six books, including **The Role of the Sangha in Modern Thailand, Tham Khwan – How to Contain the Essence of Life, Trance and Healing in Southeast Asia Today,** *and numerous essays in professional journals. She is National Director of Independent Scholars of Asia; editor of the Asian Folklore Studies Group; Northern California Representative of the Fulbright Alumni Association; on the Board of Directors of the Saybrook Institute and of a Burmese meditation center. Since 1974, she has been Research Associate at the Center for South and Southeast Asian Studies, University of California, Berkeley, and since 1984, Professor at the California Institute of Integral Studies, San Francisco. She organizes and conducts the "Universal Dialogue" workshop series as well as annual conferences on shamanism and healing.*

My family lived in Berlin which, at that time, was the capital of Germany and a big city. When I was still of pre-school age, we went to the Baltic Sea in summer. One day, I found myself alone, standing on the beach. The sea touched the sky and there I was, breathing with the waves. I entered the rhythm of the waves. There was a sudden channeling of energy – the sun, the wind, the sea – going right through me. I became the sun, wind, and sea. There was no "I" anymore for "I" had merged with everything else. A door opened. All sensory perceptions became one. Sounds, smells, tastes, shapes, melted into brilliant light. The pulsating energy went right through me. I was part of this energy.

This was the first time I got a glimpse of what shamans experience. They learn how to tap this energy and offer themselves to become the channels through which the energy can flow.

I could not talk about this experience. My parents thought I had a heat stroke and so kept me in bed, in the dark, for a couple of days. This gave me time to reintegrate and return to my family.

As a child, I did not know what to do with this vision. There was no one with whom I could talk about it, since people would think I was crazy. However, every time I have similar experiences, I remember the first time. That experience became a measuring rod for me as to whether future visions were genuine or just fictions of my imagination.

I asked my mother about whether anyone in our family had "unusual" faculties. She mentioned that her father, my grandfather, had been a healer. (He died more than twenty years before I was born, so I never met him.) When I was sixteen, I went to a village in West Prussia where my mother and my grandfather had lived at the end of the last century. It is now deep in Poland. When I walked through the village, a woman came up and said, "Your grandfather helped me. Come, let me show you my house!" She had not known about my coming but she had picked me out immediately, over forty years after my grandfather's death. When I was out of my teens and could talk to my mother more easily, she admitted that she had had some psychic experiences as well. So the openness toward the supernatural had manifested before in my mother's line.

I was educated very strictly. I had to obey without questioning and there was great concern about displaying acceptable behavior. It was not acceptable to claim to be a shaman or a healer. Somehow I felt myself that it was not right to talk about it. People would find me on their own. Relatives and friends, sometimes even strangers, came to me when they had pain. They asked me to massage them and to lay on my hands.

My mother told me that my grandfather never asked for money when he was healing. People brought him presents and food, but he never looked at what they brought or whether they brought anything at all.

When I shared the healing energy with people, I sometimes found flowers or a beautiful stone on my table after they had gone. I didn't dream of making a living out of helping people. My feeling was, how could one make a business out of a faculty which had been given to me to share? But I did need a "profession" to pay my rent.

The reason I became an actress was that I needed the stage to give all aspects of myself a chance to manifest. My daily life had been restrictive. Becoming an actress was a process of liberation. Inhibitions to show compassion dissolved, my sensitivity for others increased, the barriers between the inner and outer world became transparent. Acting was an experience of conscious expansion. I felt that all those different characters on stage were me, too. I became a "professional" actress.

In Germany, we had a kind of actors' union in which one had to take an entrance exam before becoming admitted to study. I failed the first test because my energies were boiling over, and then I passed the second exam with honors. There are so many factors involved in exams: anxiety, politics, personality clashes with the committee. They can either like you or hate you. It is quite healthy to fail once in a while in your endeavors, because with each failure your convictions are tested. Through experience you learn when to increase your efforts, and when to refine your approach. For two years I studied with a prominent actress. I took fencing and dancing lessons, and I learned how to project, and how to transform in shifting consciousness. I again failed the first final exam but passed the second with honors.

I had applied to several examination boards in Germany and Austria. Then, one day, I got a notice to appear the next morning in Vienna. I was in Berlin, so I took the night train to Austria. I did not sleep a wink. For eighteen hours I stood at the window of my compartment, repeating all my parts: eight leading ones, and about six smaller ones. I did not sit down and I did not sleep. At the examination site, in an old Austrian castle, I had to wait another three hours before I was called in. I was one of the last candidates. Emotionally and physically exhausted, I selected a dramatic scene from the "Bride of Messina," by Schiller, where a mother finds the corpse of her son. This was risky because a famous Viennese actress, Charlotte Wolters, was known for her outstanding performance of this scene. After I had finished, there was silence in the auditorium. A few minutes elapsed, and then I was asked to perform my second elective. I chose a scene from "Mary Stuart," also by Schiller, a monologue by Queen Elizabeth, that is very subdued, reflective and modern, in contrast to the earlier dramatic outcry. Having completed my performance, I stood on stage, frozen by the apparent unresponsiveness. Finally somebody asked, "Why don't you come down?" "I have failed again," was all I could think. I placed myself in front of the committee and told them, "I have to know your verdict." They laughed. Somebody realized, however, that my face was white and I was close to fainting. This person had mercy and declared, "Of course, you passed." Through lack of sleep, food, and water, my defenses had worn thin. I had opened myself to an "energy" that channeled through me and carried me in such a way that I had only to provide the form.

Throughout my seven years as a professional actress in Germany, every performance was a "wedding night." I merged with the expectations of the audience and guided them through the "experience." When one radiates the energy, one can encourage and carry others on "the journey." This is very fulfilling, because it becomes a complete experience. The physical theater turns into the theater of the universe, where pain as well as ecstacy become transparent and gain meaning on this shamanic flight.

After I had discovered how to access the energy, I had to learn how to use it. This has remained a constant process for me.

When Hitler came to power in 1933, I was thirteen years old. The torchlight marches of the storm-troopers, on the day of the take-over, are still engraved in my mind. A wall of fire came towards me. It was the fire of destruction. There was the feeling of doom. Living under a dictatorial government one has to learn to cope. One learns how to defend life, and everything that is precious. One can commit suicide, or die in the process of speaking out, or learn how to raise an invisible shield. At that time there was no one to teach us how to create that shield. We had to listen to our inner voices. When World War II started in 1939, a confrontation with death as a direct physical threat closed in on us. We, as civilians in Germany, had to enter a dialogue with death. We allowed ourselves to die inwardly, even though none of us wanted to go through the experience. Our survival instincts, our autonomic nervous system tried to protect us. Our minds, our emotions, and everything else had to face death.

Air raids started in Berlin in November, 1942. For two and a half years, Berlin was attacked by air three times a day, and at least three times each night. During the day we would leave the house, carrying our most precious belongings in a satchel. Each time, we did not know whether we would find the house still intact and those we loved still alive when we returned in the evening, or whether we would return at all. There was time neither to relax nor to sleep. Three times each night we were called by the air-raid sirens. We got up and walked down to the air-raid shelter, in the basement of our apartment house. One bomb hit the pavement in front of our house and other, incendiary bombs fell through the roof to the third floor, where I spent the rest of that night attempting to stall the fire by throwing buckets of water on it. The tenants of our house formed a chain of buckets, because the fire department could not keep up with the conflagration around us. There was no one to help us. We had to do what we could for ourselves.

In my own struggle for survival I developed a visualization to help me deal with the constant threat of death. I used a visualization that I found out years later is practiced by Tibetan Buddhists, and by shamans. I visualized death in all its aspects, the horrifying and beneficial aspects. I became death. I experienced dying. I passed the threshold to different levels of existence. I let go of my flesh, my bones, my feelings, perceptions, and thoughts. I gave myself up completely. On a philosophical level, the Buddhists talk about the sacrifice of the ego. Going through the process of dying consciously is like signing a contract with death. One remains aware of the presence of death every second. In the Bible, Abraham invented a god in the desert so that he could draw up a contract with him. I think the moment when I surrendered the fear of death was the moment of my contract and my most important initiation. I put myself together again. I was different. I had crossed a threshold. This time marked a turning point, although I have gone through many initiations since.

I found out that some of the side effects of the death experience indeed "saved my life." After dying and putting myself together again, I knew the presence of death whenever the possibility of dying arose.

During one evening air raid in 1944, for example, the bombs started falling before I could reach the air-raid shelter. It takes several minutes before the bombs, released from high-flying planes, reach the ground. One can actually watch them falling. They kept falling, very close together, like a carpet, leaving no space for you to escape. I stayed in an entrance niche to a public building which was closed at that time. Shrapnel fragments from the anti-air-raid cannons fell like rain everywhere. Hundreds of guns, big and small, kept shooting at the multitude of planes. The entrance niche barely offered any cover. Suddenly, however, I felt compelled to go out on the street and run to the next house, approximately one hundred yards away. It was a miracle that I was not hit by any of the shrapnel pieces which were falling all around me. The moment I reached the next building, the first house where I had been standing was hit by a bomb and completely demolished. I had somehow sensed the course of the oncoming bomb.

Signs of approaching death kept coming. The signs reminded me of my alliance with death, of not obstructing transformation, but my commitment to aid in avoiding blind destruction when possible. I was also called to aid people in the process of their transformation, whether they were physically present or not. I will give one example.

Four years after the war I had refused all invitations for Christmas Eve. Christmas is for me the most joyful and also the most intimate event of the year. The light is born in the middle of darkness. I was an actress at that time, performing at a theater near the German/Polish border. Because performances were scheduled during the holidays, I could not be with my family in Berlin. I planned to use the first free hours in months to relax and to meditate. I wanted to "take inventory" of myself.

I wanted to experience again the peace of mind which is so necessary for being productive. I was not avoiding the religious issue: though raised Lutheran, my faith is not based on Christian dogma. Many people on this earth celebrate during the time of the winter solstice, either the birth of a child in whom people set their hope, or a festival of light, which overcomes anxiety and darkness.

I lit a candle and turned on the radio. One station was broadcasting Bruch's violin concerto. This music always has a purifying effect on my mind and seemed fitting for the occasion. I do not remember all the stages of transformation I went through, but I do remember clearly that the music became the vehicle which carried me to a higher level of consciousness.

The next thing I remember is that I awoke at dawn, still feeling weightless, peaceful, and in harmony with the world around me. I realized that something had happened and that I had to write it down immediately, not to lose the content of the experience.

Whether it was a dream or a vision, I had felt that I was in a large house with many rooms. To test the reality of the experience, I pinched myself and felt the pain. I was in a house where people can stay overnight: a caravanserai or large shelter where pilgrims rest.

I was wandering through endless floors. There were many rooms, right and left, but all the doors were closed. Somebody approached me and I cannot remember whether I actually saw a human shape or just heard a human voice. I was told that I could not stay. There was no room for me. "Not yet," so said the voice. Why wasn't I supposed to be in this house which I felt myself drawn to by an unknown caller? Somebody responded to my question and tried to help me. I was given a basket which could be used for collecting fruit. Something was moving inside the basket. It was a red cat, purring and offering herself to be caressed. Was she to be my guide? As soon as I touched the red cat, the house, the basket, and the cat itself disappeared. I was then walking in a large garden, though I can't remember whether I had moved or left the house.

The garden was on a slope, bordering a lake or river. People were walking up and down, talking to each other in soft voices. It sounded like the murmur of a spring. The same sounds had been made by the purring cat. The men, women, and children did not wear ordinary clothes. They wore timeless gowns of a greyish-bluish color, which I had not seen before. Under the blinding sun, all colors in the garden faded away.

Through the bright haze, one man left the crowd and came towards me. He was an uncle of mine, the brother of my mother. I had always been attracted by his cheerful and giving personality. While he was talking with me, I suddenly realized that all the other people in the garden had already died. I recognized dead friends, relatives, and neighbors. At the same moment, I also remembered that my uncle and I were the only living beings in the garden. It seemed to be strange but there was nothing unnatural about it. I again pressed my thumbnail against my wrist to test whether I was dreaming or awake and again I felt pain.

When I asked my uncle why we were there, he led me to a building to the left of the garden. It looked like a mausoleum. When we entered, there were two sarcophagi. A neighbor who had been close to me when I was a child was resting in one of them. My uncle lay down in the other. I asked him why, but he who had talked to me so freely before continued to move his lips without me hearing a sound. It was like being under water where you can see, but where all the noises are blunted. I tried to undertand him and make myself understood, and I woke up with the effort.

After I had written down what I remembered, I put the report in an envelope, sealed it and gave it to another actor, telling him to open it only when I asked.

My work, performances and rehearsals asked for my full attention. Six weeks later, when we were having lunch at the theater's cafeteria, the mail was distributed. There was a letter from my parents. My actor friend asked me why I was so quiet. I told him to open the sealed envelope and to read the report. Then I gave him my parents' letter.

They told me that the neighbor who had been lying in one sarcophagus had died at the same hour as I had seen him that night, and that my uncle, with whom I had talked, had been rushed to a hospital to die three weeks later. I had responded to the dying thoughts of people who had not been "on my mind" for months, and who wanted me to hear their last message. This was the release they needed to transcend.

From the beginning, I felt I had a mission. The only "excuse" for surviving the horrors of war and oppression was that there was still work to be done. I always let the mission find me. One should not interfere when the ground is not ready.

On the shamanic path I have learned many things: I only use power when needed. I have learned to be protective of that power. Shamans should never show off their power, but only use it when a need arises.

I have learned to monitor shamanic energy. I can call it up and send it off again. If one would live constantly in contact with this energy it burns one up. The energy consumes everything, but one rises from each fire like a phoenix, because the energy is spiritual and immaterial, and whatever manifests and becomes material has to be periodically consumed by fire to purify the essence.

The energy can be used in many ways, but it always has to be necessary and ethically appropriate. Sometimes, for example, in the classroom or during a conversation, something annoying comes up, and I use the energy to clear the atmosphere so that we can move to more positive levels. After all, one only wastes time in confrontation.

I have also used shamanic energy to get out of the vicious cycle of fear. When, for example, Berlin was conquered by the Russian army in April 1945, the first eight days were complete chaos. The soldiers could do anything they wanted, in addition to plundering. Two Russian soldiers cornered me inside our house. They uncocked their guns and trained the barrels on me. If I had shown any fear, they would have shot me. At that moment, I felt like standing on a stage with the eyes of an audience trained on me. Was I not a professional actress? Had I not proven every night that I could transform the attention of the audience? So I stood there, a center of energy by myself, and smiled. It is very hard to shoot somebody who is smiling. The level of attention shifted. The soldiers went away and apparently did not know why. I had scattered their thought patterns.

How did I cultivate the energy? It was my acting teacher who first taught me diaphragm breathing. I learned to "project" with my breath. This gave me a good foundation. The air was shooting like an arrow out of my mouth and I could direct this energy wherever I wanted.

Twenty-eight years later, I meditated with an abbot in a Theravada monastery in Chiang Mai, northern Thailand. He led me gently through the basic steps. Most Westerners intellectualize too much and forget to include their body, their feelings and their spirituality. *Anapanasati* – The Mindfulness of Breathing – opens the door to other levels of consciousness. Ten years later, I went to Singapore and worked with Chinese, Malay, and Indian shamans. The Indians talked about *prana*, the Malay about the *angin*, and the Taoist Chinese about the *ch'i*. They knew how to circulate the breath and how to direct the energy to protect, to exorcise, and to heal. Being acknowledged by shamans of other cultures was very rewarding. It was also the proof that the "techniques" of using the energy are based on similar principles.

In Singapore I got the license to use Chinese herbs and practice acupuncture. I worked with a Chinese herbalist and acupuncturist in the same clinic. He was a Straits Chinese and I a German-American. Our clients were Muslim Singaporeans. When a patient entered the clinic, we used many forms of diagnosis: pulse, tongue, eye. Healing began, however, with tuning in, the healer with the patient, then both together, exploring the healing forces of nature, with information flowing back and forth.

Breath and life-force are the same. As a patient, you cleanse yourself by exhaling your repressed emotions and your pain and then you inhale the healing energies of nature. As the shaman, after you have cleansed yourself, you may inhale the unresolved problems of others, so that you can transform them, and by exhaling you share your strength with others.

Pain indicates an interrupted flow. Each process becomes too painful when we hold on to a form too tightly. Many people resist transformation. We have to let go with each exhalation. Each breath has, therefore, a double function. Exhaling has a purifying and releasing function, but after you have been fortified and replenished, you share the positive energies with others on each exhalation. Inhaling, you can draw away the negativity from others in critical moments. In moments of relaxation you receive nourishment from nature with each inhalation. The energies you channel go full cycle. If you have entered the flow, you will naturally expel destructive qualities and be nourished by the pure ones.

To have subtle energies available is useful, not only for becoming more confident but also for self-defense. Women should never depend on physical energies alone. Being sensitized to energy exchanges provides one with a surrounding radar system. This radar system has stood the test for me. Over the years, for example, I could have been assaulted at three different occasions. None of my assailants could hold me. The first one sprang at me from the back when I relaxed my defenses. He tried to claw me down, but I used the energy shield and he fled. Now, I have my "radar system" working even while I am sleeping. If something unfamiliar occurs in my vicinity, I wake up and check.

Sometimes I feel overextended. Whether secretary, organizer, translator, author, actress, producer, or most of all, teacher, all these roles occupy much of my time. It is therefore essential for me to step out of space and time, to purify myself by occasionally clearing the channels. Every time I return to "active" life, the purpose of my actions has become clearer.

I am writing more to increase my range of communication. For example, outside support came from a Fulbright-Hays research grant to study shamanism in Asia. For over ten years now, I have been conducting a workshop series, "The Universal Dialogue." I am also organizing local, national, and international conferences on the study of shamanism and alternative techniques of healing, with participants from all over the world. These conferences are testing grounds for innovative ideas which are then presented to the public. In

1984, during my conference on "The Art of Healing," representatives from different traditions – Chinese/Taoist, Tibetan/Buddhist, Indian/Ayurvedic, Islamic, Christian, Judaic, American Indian, Basque – met for the first time. Serving as a catalyst and sharing is important to me.

The learning continues. Each experience adds to and reinforces the knowing, such as my work with the people of Nias, who live very close to the "source," the Batak at Lake Toba (Sumatra), the trance mediums at the slopes of Bali's volcanoes, the hill-tribe shamans in northern Thailand, the Shinto priests at the Ise Shrine in Japan, and the shaman who practises on the twenty-sixth floor of a high-rise building in Singapore.

Each dream, vision and journey carries a message. The following visions may speak for themselves.

When I went through the earth, it did not take long to reach the other end of the tunnel. A bird was waiting for me. It was larger than an eagle. It began flying over me and circling around me. I felt it was protecting me. While watching the bird, I realized that I was flying too. Once I flew over the bird and then the bird was flying over me. Finally, we flew side by side. All of a sudden, I was driving down an American highway. There were the outskirts of a city. The many signs right and left announced things I did not need. I wished myself off this highway.

There was a gust of wind and I went with it, hitting cloud formations. The clouds covered the source of brilliant light, but they moved fast and kept changing form. Emerging from the clouds, I saw in the distance the silhouette of a city. When I came closer it turned out to be a congregation of birds. They flew up and I followed them. Everywhere, animals and humans were moving towards a center. It was a huge crater, filled with glowing red lava. People and animals jumped into the fiery lava and disappeared. I thought, "That's the melting pot! That is reincarnation!" I jumped in too and felt the molten rock inside my bones. It felt good. I became the fire, leaving no residue. When called back by the drum, I crash-landed in the center of a blossoming flower.

I saw a huge missile coming toward me. There was no way to escape. I did not resist and the missile went right through me. I did not feel any pain. Everything was consumed by the fire.

I was walking in darkness into the boundless universe. At first, the immense pitch-darkness was threatening, but then I realized that the brilliant light was behind me. Infinite light was touching my shoulders and the back of my head. There were others. We all were carrying the light into the darkness.

Each experience strengthens my mission. Every morning, the rising sun reminds me of the duty to transform negativities wherever they are encountered and to carry the light into each suffering to find the meaning.

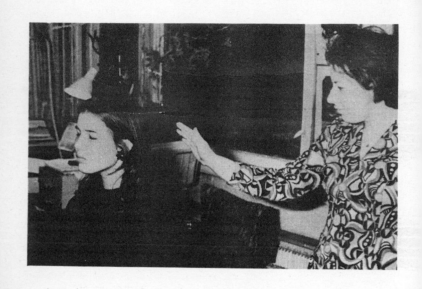

Profile 7

Larissa Vilenskaya

Larissa Vilenskaya, MA Engineering, was born in Latvia, Russia. She is a psychic researcher, healer, fire-walker, and conductor of fire-walking workshops in the US and in Europe. She is the publisher and editor of **Psi Research – An East-West Journal on Parapsychology, Psychotronics and Psychobiophysics**.

I well remember the story about a wise man and his student. "This is your knowledge," said the wise man to the student, drawing a circle. "It's small, and its outline, which touches the unknown beyond it, is also small. This is my knowledge." He drew a larger circle. "It's larger, but it touches more of the unknown beyond it." My circle of knowledge is small, and I try to make it larger. But perhaps I can reveal something to those whose circle is a bit smaller.

I was born in Riga, Latvia, when it had already become a part of Russia or, more exactly, the Soviet Union. I finished high school in a green Ukranian town, Poltava. In high school I was a bit of an oddball – other girls with their interests in boys, fashionable clothes and dancing seemed to me very superficial and often boring. Instead, I became deeply interested in unusual, extraordinary phenomena, especially those associated with the human mind. I preferred, instead of going to a party, to sit somewhere in a corner with an obscure book dug up in the local library. With great interest I made my way through a quite technical work by engineer Bernard Kazhinsky, *Biological Radio Communication*, a more popular one by Leonid Vasiliev, Professor of Physiology at Leningrad University, *Mysterious Phenomena of the Human Psyche*, and later, during my first year in college (an engineering college in Moscow), found Vasiliev's

83

major scientific publication, *Experimental Studies in Mental Suggestion.*

In 1967 I witnessed a lecture-demonstration by Karl Nikolayev and Yuri Kamensky, the well-known telepathic team, with whom Soviet scientists have been working for some time. The test was made in two different rooms. It was a kind of ESP test, in which Kamensky was given an object to send to Nikolayev telepathically. It was some sort of metal chain or necklace. But a friend of mine had an interesting idea: maybe we could interfere with the session and send our own image. The idea was to prove whether this was a stage performance, magic tricks, or whether we were really seeing the interaction of human minds.

Nikolayev was isolated in a distant room and my friend and I decided to concentrate on sending him the image of a magnet. For several minutes we concentrated on a magnet I had brought by chance from the physics lab. I imagined Nikolayev standing behind me and looking at the magnet over my shoulder. Of course we had no way of knowing what the psychic was reporting; the results of the experiment were known only after the demonstration had been concluded.

Everything Nikolayev said in the other room was transcribed. Afterward we found out that he began by describing the necklace – long, thin, metal, golden-colored – but then he began to describe our magnet as rectangular, metal, gray-silver, its approximate size and so on. Then later he went back to the necklace. This proved to us that we could interfere with a telepathy experiment and make a successful "telepathic transmission."

This event led me to serious interest in psi phenomena and para-psychology. I went to the Laboratory for Bioinformation at the A.S. Popov Scientific and Technological Society for Radio Engineering and Communication in Moscow, first as a volunteer and later as the head of the lab's Experimental and Training Group. Soon I was fortunate enough to work with Rosa Kuleshova who specialized in "fingertip vision" or "eyeless sight." It was fascinating to observe Rosa identifying colors with her fingers even when the samples were placed under several layers of opaque paper, and I myself did not know the colors. But even more fascinating was to know that Rosa had *learned* this ability through persistent exercises while working with the blind. I began toying with the idea that I could develop similar powers – from the very beginning of my attempts to study these "extraordinary qualities" I came to the conclusion that researchers of psi phenomena should not only study these abilities in others, but try to develop them in themselves.

I tried, and although I can't say I learned to read with my fingers, I was successful at identifying colors, large letters and drawings. Soon I started training others in this kind of "dermo-optic perception." While most of the girls in my group eventually learned some degree of "skin vision," the main outcome of the project was more interesting.

In 1969, shortly before working with Rosa Kuleshova, I became a student of a "psychic" healer, Sergei Vronsky, who was also working at the Laboratory for Bioinformation. I was twenty-one at that time, very shy and unsure of myself. Vronsky assured me that he could see whether people had the ability to heal and that I could do healing through the laying-on of hands if I committed myself to learning and sympathizing with other individuals' suffering. He taught us various visualization techniques and directed us to concentrate on a sense of energy flowing through the hands.

"If the patient suffers from a headache," Vronsky coached his students, "you may imagine the headache as a fog and relieve the patient of it by thinking of dispersing the fog and using the energy of your hands to achieve this." I first attempted to use this technique to relieve my girl-friend's headache. The girl was sitting with her eyes closed, and when I "saw" in my mental picture that all the fog was dispersed, the girl opened her eyes and, to my amazement, asked: "What've you done? It's gone!" Later I came intuitively to the idea of color healing, without knowing about numerous Western publications and practitioners advocating this method. This happened after my first attempts at "skin vision," when we discovered that the development of "dermo-optic perception" enhances the individual's sensitivity to the human "biological field" – the aura – and the capability to perceive colors, the structure of aura and to make diagnosis.

I began working with several persons who had previously learned "skin vision" and discovered that many of them felt a slight prickly feeling (tingling and/or vibration) while moving their hands along a human body, some five to fifteen inches from it. This, we believed, was produced by an interaction between the person's hand and the human "biofield" (aura). We learned that a person with no complaints has a biofield which is more or less regular – even or predictable. But when the patient had some disorder, my students and I felt a distortion (disequilibrium) in the "energy field." Most often we could not explain it in medical terms for all of us had little medical knowledge. At that time I began to give talks about psychic phenomena and healing. When the talk was for a non-medical audience, I usually avoided demonstrations of diagnosis and healing, since I did not want to turn my presentation into something like a circus performance. But while lecturing for a medical audience, I often successfully demonstrated diagnosis by pointing out where the patients had problems – inflammations, tumors, ulcers, scars from previous operations, etc. Although I was interested in the possibilities which this kind of diagnosis seemed to open and I liked to be able to help people, I was more intrigued with a much broader possibility – to show people their hidden potential. As I said to myself: "We all are clairvoyants, we all are healers, we just need to allow ourselves to see, to feel, to experience."

Interestingly enough, when I came up with these experiences in aura-diagnosis, I was completely unaware of similar attempts. Still, I wanted to share my observations and so I wrote a brief article which was published in the British *International Journal of Paraphysics* in 1976. Later, it was extensively quoted in Stanley Krippner's *Human Possibilities* (Garden City, New York, Anchor/Doubleday, 1980, pp. 257–9). I was astonished when many years later I came across a description of shamanic diagnosis in Michael Harner's *The Way of the Shaman*:

The shaman may use a technique that is something like employing a divining rod. . . . With his eyes closed, he stretches out his free hand back and forth over the patient's head and body, slowly discovering if there is any special sensation of heat, energy, or vibration coming from any localized point in the patient's body. By passing his hand a few inches above the body slowly back and forth, an experienced shaman gets a definite sensation in his hand when it is over the place where the intrusive power lies (*The Way of the Shaman*, New York, Bantam, 1982, pp. 153–4).

I believe that such "coincidences" usually suggest that one is on the "right path." Or do they?

Later I started working with Barbara Ivanova, leading parapsychological researcher and healer, in Moscow. Barbara, who has helped hundreds of individuals from various cities and towns throughout the Soviet Union to untap their healing powers, cautions us to be very careful with this kind of training:

If one has the ability to radiate "bioenergy," it is not enough to give one the right to heal. First of all, a harmonization of both patient and healer is necessary, and only afterward one may try to send the energy. There can be no lasting results without a certain ethical and moral development.

Thanks to Barbara's suggestions, I understood that it was dangerous to lead people in the development of their healing powers without simultaneous spiritual development, for the same energies might be used not only in a positive, but also in a negative direction. To lead people to spiritual development, however, was extremely difficult (if not impossible) in contemporary Russia, where ESP was called "bioinformation" and aura "biofield," and where everything was subjected to tight ideological control. While I was still pursuing my interest in many aspects of psi and self-development (hypnosis and self-hypnosis, relaxations, and so on) and continuing to give lectures on parapsychology and healing, I decided not to lead any more training groups. In my meditations, I first came to a feeling and then to the decision that I should completely change my life and leave the Soviet Union.

It took me about three painful years to obtain my exit visa from the USSR. During these years, I went through many troubles, the stress was unbearable, and I had to intentionally decrease my sensitivity and my perceptiveness. When I ultimately managed to leave (first to Israel and then to the United States) and emerged alone in a completely unfamiliar world, I felt totally exhausted, spent, and depleted – physically, mentally, spiritually. It seemed to me that I was many years behind as far as the development of my own "psychic powers" – much was lost, I thought, in this struggle for freedom. Although I tried to perform occasional healing to help friends, I did not feel like attempting to go any further, either in research or in self-development. I even stopped my meditation. When in 1981 I moved to the United States, I soon started *Psi Research* journal, an international quarterly on parapsychology and human potential studies. At that time I felt that writing was the only activity left for me. I translated articles from Russian and other languages, and interviewed psychics and researchers in the United States, Canada, Italy, and other countries.

At the beginning of 1983, I received an intriguing article from the Soviet Union. Entitled "Know Yourself," the article described a Soviet enthusiast of self-exploration, Valery Avdeyev, who demonstrated fire-walking by crossing, unharmed, a 30-foot-long bonfire glowing with coals, by acting on his firm belief in the virtually unlimited human potential. "As soon as we subject our organism to extreme conditions," he reasoned, "in addition to instinctive protective mechanisms, other specific subconscious defense mechanisms will be activated." Avdeyev described not only his first successful attempt at fire-walking, but another occasion in which he "could not bring himself to the proper state of mind" and was burned. "This second attempt taught me a great deal," he wrote. "I understood that the primary factor necessary for walking on coals was to enter a state of consciousness in which this seemed possible. One could learn not only to play the violin, to run the 100-meter dash, to swim the breast-stroke, but also to desensitize oneself to fire."

Soon I had an opportunity to convince myself that he was right by my own experience. In the Fall of 1983, I was invited to a "fire-walking workshop" in Portland, Oregon, conducted by a spiritual teacher from California, Tolly Burkan, who learned this art from a student of a Tibetan. Although Tolly promised to teach anyone to fire-walk safely in less than four hours, I came there without any intention to do something as crazy as "to walk on fire," but rather to write about the workshop for *Psi Research* journal. But when I witnessed Tolly walking on the red-hot coals, and then others – including a 12-year-old girl – who followed him, I remembered Avdeyev and asked myself, "If he could walk on those coals, if Tolly can, if others can do it, why can't I? They have the same skin and tissue as mine!" I felt that it was completely OK for me to participate. The coals, glowing bright orange, looked inviting and friendly. Suddenly I understood that I *could* do it, I *would* do it – and off I went! The coals were hot, but not unbearable – just like walking on hot sand. I felt exhilarated: "I did it! I did!"

Now I was certain: yes, fire-walking is definitely possible even for untrained individuals. At the same time, I've studied physics and I know that human tissue usually does not withstand temperatures higher than 60°C, and the temperature of the coals often exceeds 600°C (1,200–1,300°F). What forces and mechanisms, then, protect the skin from burns? I thoroughly reviewed the available literature from India, Greece, Bulgaria, Sri Lanka, the South Pacific, Africa, Indonesia and Japan. In a two-year study of Greek fire-walkers, Dr Vittoria Maganas administered medical and psychiatric work. She believes that the crucial component is a clear knowing that one will succeed: "Greek, Filipino, Islamic and Indian fire-dancers use different kinds of religious faith to achieve *the strength of absolute belief.*" It seems to me that now I understand what is happening at Tolly Burkan's fire-walking workshop. When people actually see someone doing something that seems impossible (e.g., walking on fire!), they experience an instantaneous shift in their belief system which makes it possible for them to "unlearn" their limitations and to instantaneously "reprogram" themselves. Similarly, then Rosa Kuleshova demonstrated her "skin vision" capacities and then

asked others to recognize colors or drawings with their eyes
closed, many were successful, since they just witnessed another
person performing the "impossible feat."

Previously I had demonstrated "aura diagnosis" and healing,
which led people to believe in "impossible" powers; now I
understood that I had come to possess a much more important
"tool" – to be able to show how to walk on fire. Eureka! this
was what I needed. I returned to Tolly Burkan and said to him,
"I want to study with you. I want to know everything you
know. I want to understand the art of fire-walking and to be
able to conduct such workshops."

In May 1984, I was invited to participate in a three-week
study tour with Tolly Burkan and his wife Peggy to become a
"fire-walking instructor" – to learn to conduct fire-walking
workshops. In the course of this training, Tolly and Peggy led
us not only through breathing exercises and the American
Indian sweat-lodge, but also through quite unusual tests.
Because the specific topic of Tolly's seminars is overcoming
fear and limitations through fire-walking, we, eleven trainees
(including three women), were invited to break through our
own fears and limitations. Tasks proposed to us during these
"three weeks beyond the limits" included spelunking in the
largest Californian cavern (which started with lowering
ourselves 200 feet down a rope), parachute jumping, spending
a night alone in the forest, and similar "trials." These proved to
be much more difficult for me than fire-walking, since some of
them required a certain degree of physical fitness, which I
lacked, but I still had to meet the challenge. Starting rappelling
or jumping out of a plane (I made two parachute jumps) I
thought: "I'll be in the hands of God! I know that physically I
am not ready to do something like this, but I *can* and I *will*!"

During the training, we participated in ten fire-walking
workshops and conducted some of them together as a team
with Tolly. After several fire-walks I realized that there were
no two identical fire-walks in terms of subjective feelings and
perceptions. Sometimes the coals felt quite hot, while at times
the heat was virtually imperceptible. Sometimes it was quite
easy to step on the embers, and at other times I again went

through a self-analysis like before the very first walk: "Am I ready?"

Soon, however, I came up with a "technique" which allowed me to concentrate quickly before a fire-walk. Before stepping onto the coals, I first looked down for a moment, then directly ahead and experienced a "letting go" feeling, surrendering to the "inner wisdom of my mind and body," as I often put it (conscious thoughts and doubts should not interfere). I stood in front of the pit until I felt an increase in energy (similar to preparing to perform healing) and a sudden inner impulse, "You are ready, go!" Usually it is almost impossible for me to assess how much time passes from when I come into "position" in front of the coals until I step onto them, but my friends have assured me that "my state of timelessness" does not usually last more than a few seconds. I also understood that, in order to fire-walk, I did not need to achieve "mastery" or "power" over fire. My task would be much easier if I felt one with the fire – if I am a part of it, it cannot hurt me.

I am often asked whether or not fire-walking is performed in an altered state of consciousness. It is not easy for me to answer this question: although while concentrating before a fire-walk I seem to not lose touch with the "ordinary reality," at the same time I am in another reality, "my reality," in which I am one with the fire and the fire cannot hurt me.

While our team traveled throughout the west coast of the US, I witnessed hundreds of "unprepared" people walking across beds of hot coals after three to four hour seminars with no injuries other than an occasional blister (except one person who was burned more seriously). I became interested in whether any differences could be found between those who blister and those who emerge from the fire-bed completely unharmed. My preliminary observations indicate that at least there are no obvious, easily dectectable differences: the only tendency I could pinpoint was that those who walked more confidently (not necessarily faster, often quite the opposite) got blisters more rarely. When I asked Peggy Burkan whether she had an "anti-blistering" technique, her answer was immediate: "Sometimes I get blisters too. Most important, don't go onto the fire casually! When I started getting blisters, I had to upgrade my energy." Her answer reminded me of what I read some time ago about fire-walking in Polynesia.

At the beginning of the century, Colonial Gudgeon wrote about a fire-walking ceremony in Polynesia, in which four Europeans participated. He described that the local priest (called *tohunga* in the local dialect) and his disciple came to the Europeans, and the disciple handed one of them a branch of the Ti plant (Dracaena) as the priest said to him: "I hand my *mana* (power) over to you; lead your friends across." Gudgeon, who walked on the red-hot stones unharmed, emphasized in his account: "A man must have *mana* to do it; if he has not, it will be too late when he is on the hot stone. . . . I can only tell you it is *mana — mana tangata* and *mana atua*."

Is this just one more belief that can be dismissed as easily as the notion of observing a specific diet for successful fire-walking (which is known in Greece and other countries)? Or are we again encountering this concept of "life energy" known as *prana*, *qi* or *mana*? After all, some researchers (e.g., Joseph Chilton Pearce and Andrew Weil) indicate a clear connection between fire-walking and healing:

> I agree with the fire-walkers of Greece that the *power that protects them from burns can also cure disease* [emphasis added]. The mind holds the key to healing, and healing is as extraordinary as fire-walking. It may also make use of some nervous pathways and mechanisms (Dr Andrew Weil, *Health and Healing*, Boston, Houghton Mifflin, 1983, p. 249.

Yogis maintain that *prana* heals, and Chinese *qigong* masters attribute the same quality to *qi* energy. I tend to believe that fire-walking workshops, which usually include collective singing, "*om*ing," chanting and other kinds of group interaction, lead to "focusing the energy" of the participants (if we speak in these terms) to create a unified, synergistic group energy. One of the healers whom I know well, Barbara Ivanova in Moscow, conducts mass healing sessions in which she works with the whole group in a similar way to that which she uses when healing a single patient. She believes that the "group energy field" is created during this process. Another Soviet healer, Alexander M., discusses similar ideas:

> All the actions in which human beings participate can be subdivided into individual and collective. "Collective" suggests three or more people. When it is only two, it's still a personal act. In primitive societies, it is assumed that a collective, "team" consciousness has a greater degree of power and influence. This is all based on a relatively well-known statement that a thought is an action. This confronts one of the basic questions of philosophy, "What is an action? Does the concept or idea of an action correspond to the action itself?. . . . If so, we can possibly explain the phenomena and visions that occur in team healing or team praying.

When I studied fire-walking with Tolly and Peggy Burkan, I received one more interesting hint in the same direction. The last day of our training course they conducted a type of "graduation ceremony" for our group, which included an ancient American Indian ritual with feathers. While Tolly was putting sage on burning charcoal and praying, Peggy asked us to come up to her, one by one, and moved the ritual feathers around the person, whispering something which was barely audible to the rest of the group. When I came up to her, I did not have any preconceptions or expectations as to what was supposed to happen – in fact, I respected the ritual but did not expect anything special. However, standing with my eyes closed, as was required, I felt a tremendous surge of energy through my body – the intensity of which I've never before experienced in my life. And then I heard Peggy's words: "*Take the power!*"

I agree that this concept of *external* energy leads to the same question as that asked by Dr Weil, "Why do fire-walkers from Fiji to Greece think their powers come from deities and saints rather than from their own minds?" I believe that there is no contradiction between the two approaches: we are *interconnected* with each other and with external forces and energies, known and unknown, and what is believed to be the powers of *our* minds may result from this global interconnectedness.

Soon after my apprenticeship with Tolly and Peggy Burkan, I started my own fire-walking workshops in the United States and in Europe. Now I felt much more confident: I wanted to use fire-walking as a tool, as a metaphor to lead people to overcoming fears and limiting beliefs, to healing, to psychological change and growth. "If you can walk on fire, you can do anything you choose," I repeated after Tolly. I am in total agreement with him that "nothing limits us more than fear," and although I understand that fire-walking is not the only way to become free from fear, from my own experience I see that it is effective.

These subjective opinions of the significance of fire-walking have recently been confirmed by psychologist Julianne Blake, MA, who conducted an intriguing study of psychological effects of fire-walking published in the June 1985 issue of *Psi Research* journal. Using specific psychological tests (the State-Trait Anxiety Inventory, the Internal-External Locus of Control, and the Personal Orientation Inventory) and in-depth follow up interviews of participants of fire-walking seminars, she came to conclusion, "*Firewalking is empowering!*" She found that fire-walking successfully led individuals to discounting the influence of "powerful others" and reinforced the belief in the controllability of life ("*We create our own reality*"). The prevailing attitude of those who walked on fire is:

> I finally discovered a new way of being: as a human, I possessed limitless possibilities which I had finally touched upon. I realize also that all human beings have this potential.

With recent widespread interest in fire-walking, I have also been thinking of another intriguing possibility. It has long been known that Greek fire-dancers "*consider themselves healers of all the community*." Similar beliefs and attitudes are widespread in other parts of the world where fire-walking and fire-dancing are practiced as a ritual. I am far from endorsing the claims of Transcendental Meditation (TM) advocates, that the practice of

TM by many individuals creates an inexplicable effect on the "social field" which results in reduced accidents, illness, and crime (as measured by statistical social indicators) in their communities. But, since I have become better acquainted with fire-walking, my thoughts keep returning to the possibility that fire-walking has equal potential to play this role. After all, many ancient legends and rituals have already been found to be based on facts, rather than on people's imagination. Why not another one?

I believe that studying fire-walking (both traditional and contemporary practices) will lead to a better understanding of the mechanisms of "psychic" healing and self-healing, especially in the light of the above suggestions by J.C. Pearce, A. Weil and others that "fire-walking involves the same process as innate healing." Now all my interests have come together: along with conducting fire-walking seminars, I started again teaching "energy" or "psychic" healing (some of my healing seminars end with a fire-walk). I am also happy to see that many participants at fire-walking seminars are extremely interested in exploring the spiritual implications of fire-walking and regard the seminar as a profound spiritual experience. At the same time, most of the participants clearly understand that fire-walking is by no means the ultimate goal, but just the beginning to self-exploration, personal transformation, and a better understanding of ourselves, our consciousness, and the universe.

I believe in human potential, potential of free individuals to find missing links within ourselves, between ourselves, and with the world beyond which we know very little about.

Profile 8

Petey Stevens

Petey Stevens is the co-director of Heartsong, a school of psychic and healing development in Albany, California. She is the author of **Opening Up to Your Psychic Self**, *a primer on psychic development. She has been on several national television shows, conducting psychic experiments with the audience. Petey has had formal psychic training, but most of her shamanic training has come through communications and trance-channelings from the spirit world.*

From the time I was a very little girl I had always thought about healing the world. How to realistically participate in this dream did not enter my life until after the birth of my first child in 1971. Now that I look back at the first years of her life, I realize that the many hours I spent breastfeeding were some of the only hours I spent sitting still and going within. The breastfeeding ritual itself created a "forced" meditation time for me. This opened me up to the more subtle realities around me. As I looked into Heather's eyes I knew that I had something to do with her sweet little body, but there was a spark of essence in there that had nothing to do with me. Sometimes I would see a very small baby girl and other times I would see an ancient wise man. When asked her age I would tease, "Nine months going on one hundred and nine months." I grew in ways that I had never imagined. My heart was so full of joyful love and my mind overflowed with ways to give my devotion. There grew a correctness within me and I knew that I was doing exactly what I was supposed to be doing – mothering this tiny human being and pondering the effects of love, goodness and life in general.

I grew to love my meditations. I allowed my time to be

governed by Heather's needs and fit the meditations into her schedule. If I didn't resist motherhood and the housework, I could go into a fairly deep trance while getting the floor swept or the bathroom washed. My existence as mother and home-maker became my "dharma" and my housework became my "mantra."

I felt as if I were holding onto a big secret but I wasn't quite sure what it was! It had something to do with truth and clear communications and quite possibly the human soul. At first I didn't know what to do with this huge shift in my reality and world-view. Then I heard a voice as clear as could be say to me, "Move to Berkeley. You will find your answers there."

Berkeley in the early 1970s was Mecca to me. The timing coincided with my Saturn cycle and Comet Kohoutek's visit to our solar system. It was all very special and significant for me. Starving for information and companionship along the pathway I had chosen, I was drawn to classes and teachers to study mind control and metaphysics. I attended many classes and went as deep into my soul as the teachers would take me. This obsession of mine was growing into a process, an opening and flowering of my true nature and the emergence of my soul. After many classes and many meditations, I was beginning to understand that my body was a vehicle for my soul to manifest in a particular space and time. I was like a sponge soaking up every bit of information I could find dealing with anything paranormal and the soul. Many of the classes led me to the study of psychic phenomena. The word psychic was in harmony with me. It comes from the Greek word "psychicos" which means "of or pertaining to the soul" and this was exactly what my journey was . . . a journey of the soul.

Pretty soon during my meditations I started to astrally project into my past and review early personality patterns and childhood programming. I was astonished to find that much of my life was distracted or affected by the opinions of others. Many unanswerable feelings and events in my life began to fit together. Often it was like finding a piece to an old, unfinished puzzle. For one example, I always cried easily. It was both interesting and healing for me to know that I was taking on other peoples' emotions and feeling them. As a child I had been called "over-sensitive" or "over-emotional." Those labels never helped me understand my behavior. I now realize that there is no such thing as "over-sensitive." That was someone else's reaction to my sensitivity. There are many degrees of sensitivity and mine was acute and intense. I was an out-of-control healer trying to take on and process everyone's problems and emotions. I needed to let go of the negativity around my sensitivity, learn to make a separation from others and mostly learn to control my psychic energy.

"Running" or moving energy deliberately through my channels gave me much more control. It became obvious to me that negative programming about myself and the world "hung out" in an aura around my body and that I was filtering every experience through this programming. Unpeeling these old programs became my every-day work. As programs that created a dissonance in my aura were dissolved, I began to know my own psychic energy. A side effect of dissolving these negative beliefs was the concurrent renewal of self-love. As many of the destructive behavior patterns previously worn were shed, I discovered their origins were other people's opinions and considerations and not mine at all!

The soul's perspective gave me autonomy. It empowered me! My heart felt warm and my head was clear. I began to understand how I could consciously create my own reality which enabled me to take more responsibility for my life. My healing and opening process was underway and I wanted to share psychic awareness with everyone.

During 1973 I studied at the Berkeley Psychic Institute for their six-month advanced program. Immediately following, I was hired to teach their advanced program, which I did for nine months. Having found myself dissatisfied with some of the school's policies and attitudes, I ventured out on my own. I was determined to offer the community a school with high ethical standards and a compassionate heart.

I have always enjoyed working with a soul mate, so, for me, it was only natural when I met Rick Stevens to both marry him and start a school with him. Rick had gone through the Institute also (after much convincing!). Our relationship was turbulent, passionate, complementary and competitive. Yet even through this diversity our unique combination was always creative. Our personalities were very different and when it clicked for us it was perfect; when it didn't click it was war. Rick is quite intellectual by nature and had an understanding of the inner workings of a school which lent my ease and command of the work a professional air. Our souls met at the need for high ethical standards enhancing personal autonomy and integrity. It was a good combination, and Heartsong was born. So were Solomon, Sarah, and Cassie, giving Heather a full family of siblings.

Once Heartsong was started there was no stopping it. Heartsong came from the center of my heart. I was devoted. Yet I was also devoted to my growing family, so I combined my jobs – mother and Heartsong director – by placing an off-premise extension to Heartsong's phone in my kitchen. That way I was able to be there for my little children and answer the Heartsong phone at the same time. I personally do not think I would have made it through those early baby years without Heartsong. It was a creative outlet for me. I loved teaching and got such enthusiasm in return that it made some of those "all-nighters" with sick children easier to survive. The opposite was also true. Even when Heartsong was its most difficult, I always had my loving little ones giving me hugs and kisses. I guess that it has always been a comfortable balance for me between work and family.

Having the phone in the kitchen presented some funny and seemingly impossible situations. One time I was dumping the garbage and heard the Heartsong phone ring. I thought it would be best answered by the answering machine. When I got inside, Sarah, three years old and terribly independent, was carrying on a conversation about Heartsong with a client. Another recurring scenario was when all my children would be laughing, joking, fighting, crying or dancing in the kitchen when the Heartsong phone would ring. As if well rehearsed, all the children would instantaneously be quiet. I would then answer the phone quite formally and take up my role as Heartsong's director. Just as miraculously, the exact second I'd hang up the phone they would start up again as if the call had never happened. I truly appreciate my children's respect and cooperation with the creation of Heartsong.

Setting up the school was a joy to me. I loved creating teaching modules to develop specific psychic abilities. Rather quickly we gathered excellent teachers and very capable students. We spent countless hours meditating, meeting, developing ideas and executing visions. Rick took on the enormous task of obtaining our church non-profit status from the state and federal governments. As for me, my enthusiasm for the work kept my heart inspired. Rick and I were the head and heart of Heartsong, respectively. This formula worked well for some time.

It is so wonderful to be on my own pathway! I never tire of the work. It feeds a very deep part of my soul. When I give a reading, the process of "seeing" helps clear me of stuck programs. Also when I channel a healing the healing energy racing through my channels helps heal me. After completing five or six hours of sessions and classes I will often feel elated rather than exhausted. I see every session, every class and every TV show as both a chance to communicate and a continuing process of learning how to communicate this ancient wisdom to the modern world. Quite often yesterday's magic is today's experiment and will become tomorrow's science. This is definitely true for psychic work.

It was finally revealed to me that I had not been doing this spiritual journey alone. One day while I was reading my *I Ching,* a large Chinese spirit voice boomed in my head, "Can I be direct with you?" Not knowing what else to say, I said "Yes" so he explained himself to me. It seemed that I had inherited a group of spirit guides back in the 1960s along with the *I Ching* book. Although I was unaware of their presence, the guides were at work with my best interests in mind. To speak to me they would intercept the Chinese coins as I threw them. The coins would create the hexagram that the guides wanted me to read. Certain throws guided major decisions in my life and in Heartsong's life. We both get certain recurring hexagrams. I seem to get "Enthusiasm" over and over. Reading it has always brought me back to my largest gift . . . my enthusiasm. The hexagram also reminds me to use song and tones to bring me back to that enthusiasm. The staff at

Heartsong have all gotten both "The Creative" and "The Fellowship of Men" many times when throwing for the school. "The Creative" reminds us of the neutrality and non-conditional yet vital and fertile force at our disposal. "The Fellowship of Men" suggests exactly its own meaning. Heartsong has always been co-created by its members.

As I gained more confidence with spirit, it became obvious to me that I had some deeply rooted fears, not of this world. During my meditations and readings I realized that there was a portion of my aura that looked like an upside-down black pyramid. Not only was this part of my aura in another time, but it was also on another level of consciousness, the astral level. The answer to this puzzle was unlocked in my childhood nightmares. I had visions of monsters that plagued my dark room. To protect myself I finally learned to shut down my clairvoyance. After all, if I didn't "look," I wouldn't have to "see." This astral blindness was clouding my view of the world. My sixth chakra, or third eye, was completely blocked by fear and these creatures were a part of it. I had been teaching and reading by feeling and knowing the energy but not "seeing" it. During a deep trance I witnessed the block. It was like a movie, an old movie with a flickering light effect at first. When the picture smoothed out I could "see" as if I were in a movie theater. It was Egypt and I was being buried alive. My Egyptian husband had died and wanted to take me with him into the nether world. Although it was customary for the wife of a ruler to be ritualistically killed, mummified and buried with the dead ruler, my death had been intercepted. Instead, I was loosely bound in my mummy's cloth, then placed in a casket and buried alive in the tomb with my husband's dead mummified body. I was supposed to get out of the casket and meet a friend just before the last stone was placed. In all my terror and frenzy to get out of there, the cloths around me had gotten stuck somehow on something near the casket, and I missed the rendezvous. By the time I got free the torches had all gone out and it was very dark. Vivid memories of decay were all round me. I remember the dank smell. My clairvoyance was lucid as I witnessed the astral levels of death and dying. I couldn't discern at what point my body died and subsequently stayed in the tomb among the living dead for centuries.

That past-life memory came into my consciousness when I was only two years old. I would repeatedly get out of bed at bedtime. This disrupted my parents' schedule, so they tried everything to keep me in bed, including the use of a harness to strap me to the crib. This harness brought back the memory of my Egyptian life, and I had been "stuck" in fear and memory for years. Freeing myself of the terrible death I experienced in Egypt brought my vision back! I could "see" again! Every day I gained more control of my clairvoyance. I no longer feared those lower astral levels. Instead of monsters, I started "seeing" old Felix the Cat and Farmer Brown cartoons. Later I found out that many sprouting clairvoyants have a phase of "cartooning." After this short-lived phase passed, I started to "see" many forms of psychic energy. I saw auras around everyone's body. A whole new visual world had opened to me.

Past-life connections with my children kept popping up all the time. Once I was telling a friend about my Egyptian experience when my son, Solomon, who was seven at the time, overheard. When I got to the part about the casket, Solomon said, "Mom, I did a bad thing. I carried your casket and I could feel your live body move and I didn't tell anyone." Solomon and I instantly became aware of our souls' eternal connections. We hugged and laughed and forgave each other.

The meditations that followed the birth of my fourth child concentrated around writing a book. I fought against it at first. "After all," I said to myself, "I am the heart, not the head." Rick had always talked about writing a book, so at first I believed that I was betraying him or our relationship by becoming an author. I kept trying to not do it and the information kept channelling through despite my attempts at stopping it. After a while the channellings were bigger than both of us and I started to write a primer on psychic development called *Opening Up to Your Psychic Self*. Rick took over all the administrative work at Heartsong and also helped much more with the home and children. I let a lot of the housework go that year. When the children would leave their toys around the house, instead of putting the maverick toys away I would place them in a box. I had five large boxes of these toys by the end of the year!

Most of the bulk of *Opening Up* was written between seven at night and four in the morning, plus any moment I could steal during the day, often with Cassie on my breast. My children seemed to understand my need to write *Opening Up*, and for that I bless them. One of my students gave me a tape to which I credit the focus necessary to be both full-time mother and author at the same time. It was called *Tibetan Bowls and Bells II*, by Wolff and Hennings. It had a hypnotic effect on me. I played it flip-side to flip-side, over and over again. Each time I would sit down to write, no matter how noisy or scattered the room I came from was, the minute I heard the tape I was brought right back to where I had left off with complete focus and awareness.

During the creation of *Opening Up* I became intensely interested in energy healing. Heartsong already had a full healing program started by a very capable lady named Elizabeth Chrisler-Harris and continued by other capable healers. When my book was complete, an opening arose at the school and I took over the healing program. I loved it. It was a new territory for me. Each day I would look forward to doing healings with the advanced students. We were all pioneers expanding new horizons. We began to channel healing energy through our vocal tones. The results were astonishing! The sounds and tones were communicating effective and long-lasting healing energy. They came from deep within the healer and went deep within the healee. The month we first introduced tones was exam month at the University of California in Berkeley and we were full each night toning and healing "Burnt-out," fatigued students. By November of 1983 Heartsong was getting invited to do a demonstration healing and have a debate about it on television. The show won an emmy for channel seven and we shared our healing techniques with millions of viewers.

Opening Up had opened me up. Rick and I were moving in different directions and the marriage was ending. I started to gain confidence in myself in ways I had not felt before. I loved being on radio and TV and felt a resurgence of power. I had given so much of myself to Rick and was just beginning to realize it. The book *Medicine Woman* was given to me and I felt a strong sisterhood with its author, Lynn V. Andrews. As Lynn was crawling on her belly in the dirt through the forest, I was metaphorically crawling on my belly, slithering out of the laundry-room and kitchen into the living-room and into the world. While Lynn got her marriage basket from Red Dog, I was regaining control of my life. I was taking back the power that I had so freely given the men in my life.

My spirit guides told me that this power was not the only part of my self that I had to reclaim. In order to gain enough power to create and manifest my childhood dream of helping heal the world, I was also to reclaim experiences and information from my own past-life incarnations.

The first past life I constantly visited was an Atlantean incarnation. My guides had instilled within me reverence towards my new venture. To maintain that reverence I lay down on the floor in the center of Crystal Heaven, which is a circular configuration of twelve quartz crystals. The electro-magnetic properties of the quartz crystals set up an energy field that felt as if I were being cradled in my mother's womb. Astral projection always feels better when I leave from Crystal Heaven. Then I set my personal energy and left my body: destination – my first significant lifetime on this planet. I felt that first rush of a tingling sensation all over my body and I knew that I would experience my astral projecton very soon. Everything was very white. Buildings and clothes were white. I felt myself move swiftly and lightly through the doors of a large, domed building. In front of me were long cabinets about five feet high and long aisles between. I pulled a drawer out and saw the most beautifully clear assortment of aquamarine crystals, settled into rock salt. The room was bright and had a pristine aura about it. I wondered to myself, "Are these healing tools?" I heard a reply, "Yes." I turned around and in the doorway was a woman dressed in white with a large quartz crystal on a chain around her neck. At first it was a surprise to me that she and I were going to be able to communicate so easily, but I quickly grew accustomed to her because of my desire to learn. She proceeded to teach me about the effects of crystals, tones and sunlight on the human aura. She also taught me as a woman how to be both strong and at the same time yielding. I had long felt a split between my female and male energy. Alta, my Atlantean counterpart, balanced her energy in a way that was a very comfortable addition to my present day life as Petey.

With Alta came a whole new level of healing. It is called transchannelling. During one healing session in early 1984 there was a block of energy over my client's right shoulder. I stepped back to assess the situation and Alta told me to open my mouth to tone and suggested that she come through my body to "tone out" the client's block. At first I was somewhat embarrassed by her tones. They sounded long and somewhat hollow as if they were coming out of a long tunnel. After a while I got very used to sharing my body with her during healing sessions. Since that first transchannelling I have incorporated several other past-life personalities of mine including a Montauk Indian and an Egyptian Winged Pharaoh.

The Indian's name was Laughing Water and after his arrival into my reality I became fixated on certain quartz rocks on the beach of the Little Peconic Bay at the end of Long Island. Naturally tumbled in the bay, the stones are oval and are uniform in size. They are used in pictorial configurations to evoke creative and healing energies. My parents got a laugh when they saw me pack up over fifty pounds of these stones to bring back to Heartsong!

The Egyptian Winged Pharaoh, named Nephsi, was a woman "seer" who did most of her work on the astral during dreams. It is a form of healing where the Winged Pharaoh projects out of her body and into the astral reality of another. She can easily manipulate the energy body as a chiropractor would manipulate bones to create a correctness of wholeness for the client. The client may or may not remember the astral visit. My fascination with Siamese cats started when I was ten years old. During one transchannelling, Nephsi spoke of the Siamese cats she trained to watch and protect their Winged Pharaohs during astral projections.

I do a great deal of teaching on the astral. I remember one

night I was out teaching my advanced students how to fly and the next morning a neighbor I seldom see came over to tell me that she'd had a dream about me, and that I was teaching her how to fly! In August of 1985 while being interviewed on channel four, I challenged the TV viewing audience to accompany me on an astral projection that night. Furthermore, they were to call TGI4 the next day and tell them what they'd experienced. I meditated from 12.00 midnight to 2.00 in the morning. I took many people on a directed and somewhat complex astral projection. The following day TGI4 had a hot line and their viewers called in with their experiences. It was both fun and very validating for me. I'm sure that many of these travelers had been Winged Pharaohs themselves!

After I had been transchannelling for a while, I began to experience myself as belonging to the family of God. Not quite the God I had understood as a child . . . not a male God either, nor a female Goddess, but both God and Goddess combined . . . the Aquarian Age God . . . ALL THAT WE ARE TOGETHER. My feelings towards everyone encompassed a broader base of commonality. We were all souls manifesting and focusing in time and space. I developed a more complete access to my past lives and started to recognize people I met as people I have known in different incarnations. I am usually able to feel an instant relationship with such soul beings. As past-life knowledge awakened into my present-life awareness, I began to realize that the Universe is really a University for souls to incarnate and practice manifesting with physical matter. This lifetime as Petey is just another semester and I have a great deal of spiritual work and healing to do on my own soul.

It was at this time that I met an old soul friend named Jay Menashe. He was open psychically and had been a healer for several incarnations. In this lifetime he also had a good head for business and helped me move Heartsong from a dark, somewhat hidden building in downtown Berkeley to a beautiful, open, light building on the main street in nearby Albany, where Heartsong is situated now. He also created some financial prosperity for Heartsong with a metaphysical bookstore on the first floor of the building. Heartsong currently serves about 200 students per month with readings, healings, classes, professional training programs, and planetary healing circles.

Now I am ready to take on the world! My next book is almost complete. It is called *Ten Ways to a More Psychic You*. My goal is to both educate and popularize psychic development. Surely a planet full of psychically aware people can co-create a peaceful world community. I believe that psychic development, when understood as development of the soul, offers a perspective that encourages responsibility and compassion.

A society that supports a psychic school located in a prestigious, otherwise conservative neighborhood, with a sign bearing a three-foot heart with wings (an ancient Atlantean symbol) suggesting the wings of the spirit meeting the heart of the body, is evidence of a changing world-view. It encourages me. My childhood dream of helping to heal the world has come true through Heartsong. I am certain that we can all heal the world . . . one person at a time!

> May the Wings of Your Spirit
> Meet the Heart of Your Body.

Profile 9

Vicki Noble

Vicki Noble is the author of **Motherpeace – The Way to the Goddess through Myth, Art, and Tarot**, *and is the co-designer of the Motherpeace Tarot Cards. Vicki is a teacher of the Tarot and of yoga, and is a healer and practitioner of Rosen bodywork.*

My first experience with healing was when I had an ulcer and tension headaches. I began to meditate, to change my diet, and to touch myself. It was by touching my stomach in an intuitive way that my healing was facilitated. In the bathtub at night I made little circles on my stomach with my hands. I did that because it was soothing, without having any knowledge of the healing arts. Then during one bath I placed my hands on my stomach and felt suddenly that my hand reached right inside and turned the pain into pleasure. It was an amazing tactile experience. My ulcer went away after that. It became clear to me that the healing touch was important to me and would be an important part of my work in some way.

The first of my eight years in Berkeley, California, is what I think of as my shamanistic period. During that year I started working with herbs and foods like brown rice that are really nourishing and that change the cellular structure. At that time I had started taking psychic classes, and was reading visionary literature. On Candlemas in February 1977 I had an ecstatic experience of going out of my body and into the sky. I had the feeling that I was a witch and always had been, and that I was one with all witches all over the world in a unified state. Soon after that Candlemas I had another experience.

I sat down on my bed facing a spiral African wall-hanging on my wall. The room, the walls began to undulate. The

111

center of the wall-hanging opened out. Images began to flash like a slide-show, as if it were a screen. Images of the triple Goddess, images of bulls, gargoyles and griffins – things I had never seen and didn't have any reference for.

The energy was such that I was crying at the time. I felt like I was on fire and was being visited in some way.

A tunnel opened up in the wall and beckoned. I was afraid, and said I needed a sign. Immediately a book, or a stone with some kind of language on it appeared. Since then I have come to understand that what I saw was a Runic script, but I didn't know then.

I couldn't read the script. I felt inadequate as if I were failing the test or something. The letters then reformed into English writing, saying things like "Heal all" and "Helena." Later I came to know that the name Helena was the name for aeon – of the new age. The aeon in the Tarot is the Judgment card, and my life card in the Tarot is the Judgment card. But I didn't learn any of this information until five years later. The vision was such a profound experience for me. It ended with the pulsating words: "I Am ALL," "I Am ALL."

Since then I've continued to feel the healing Presence that I experienced in my vision. I have called on the Presence in extremely critical, serious moments, when it literally cleansed my body of whatever was wrong. I also bring that energy through for inspiration such as when I hold hands in a circle with people or speak.

The energy that I experience is the Goddess, whom I feel a very personal relationship with. Some people feel the presence of guides, or an abstracted experience of the Spirit, but in my experience I literally feel the presence of the Goddess.

The Mother manifests in synchronistic ways in nature, and in the invisible forces. My classic example of that is: I was out on the porch with my husband and I was telling him about a dream that I had had in which I saw a red-tailed hawk circling above me. As I was telling Jonathan this, he and I looked up and there was a red-tailed hawk directly above us! In the Native American medicine astrology wheel written about by Sun Bear, the red-tailed hawk is my animal. I take such synchronistic experiences very literally. I read them as messages and work with them such as I would with dreams.

One of the blessings in my life is that my husband and I are shamans together. Having a partner is very exciting.

He and I sat in the woods one night. We began to see sparkles as it got dark before the moon came up, I said, "I can't believe it! I think I'm seeing the light-beings. I've never seen them before." Just little flickers . . . almost like fireflies, only more subtle. I had my hand down . . . one landed . . . then another . . . and another . . . and they painted my hand phosphorescent white-green. Then I put my other hand next to it to compare, and it was totally different. I thought this was the way the light-beings could communicate with us best. It was like no other experience I've ever had. It could have been out of a fairy-tale. When we open to the invisible, our lives become so enriched. Shamans all over the world experience this side of reality all the time.

There are many aspects to my shamanic experience, and my sexuality is an important part of it. My experiences of my sexual energies are very sacred and always have been. I've been disappointed in any casual sexual experience. Because sexuality itself is so sacred, and the commune with the other person so holy, a casual encounter has always been superficial and distracting for me.

The higher the fire burns, the more I know the Divine. It's as if we meet in ecstacy. I have learned that this path is called Tantra. It's the path of female sacred sexuality.

Orgasms are very inward. The clitoris is a very inwardly focused organ. Sexual activity causes an energy to move up through the body. It naturally raises it to a higher power. The more orgasmic a woman is – at least this has been my experience – the higher the energy goes.

Out of that sexual experience for a woman comes intuitive ability, creativity – a kind of sacred understanding of the cosmos. It's like taking a psychedelic drug where you really open and see with your third eye. All women have this potential power in their bodies. I don't think we have to go through twenty years of rigid ascetic techniques to find it. I think it's only hidden from us.

The priestesses of the ancient times were whole women.

They were whole beings. The priestess was a sacred healer who did her healing through her sexuality. She was a sexual teacher who provided a spiritual initiation through that path.

When patriarchy crystallized about five thousand years ago, the sacred women became "harlots," "whores," today's "sluts." The patriarchal mind-set split the female archetype in two. The "Madonna/whore" syndrome was invented by the patriarchal mind-set. It is a false splitting of the female. The "virgin/priestess," which meant a woman who belonged to herself, was perverted into "prostitute" which means someone, a woman, bought.

The chaste mother or the holy mother was turned into a drudge. She is someone who is owned. All women suffer I believe from this split. Inside ourselves we intuit the sacred sexual woman self. It's here within our form. It's here within our body. The sacred mother, the sacred lover, is a woman who is not split or fragmented.

I came to these realizations as a result of research I did on women's history, and as a result of my own experiences and reflections. The first thing that I did with the knowledge and the kind of coherence it was beginning to have for me is that I started to teach what I call Lunar Yoga. It was a very different yoga than was ordinarily taught. I invited people to take a class with me for free, because my form of yoga was so unusual that I thought they had better know what they were getting into.

I used to teach my yoga classes in a low light with candles. I worked intensely with energy. Every time we did a hatha yoga posture I would let people know the effects it would have on the physical body, and on the spiritual entity.

During the period of teaching Lunar Yoga, I discovered Tarot cards. I immediately saw that the Goddess teachings had survived within that form. However, the Tarot had patriarchal interpretations superimposed on it. The Waite deck is the standard, traditional Tarot that most people are familiar with. It works as a symbol system, but it's so sterile that female sexuality has been removed from it. The Crowley Tarot deck, on the other hand, is very magical and powerful in its imagery, and has a lot of female sexuality portrayed, but it has a very biased male projection of what female sexuality is. All the sexual energy in the images are somehow distorted interpretations of the Tantras. Female sexuality in the cards is presented as being something for men and for Crowley. Similarly, there are books on the market that talk explicitly about the Tantric discipline being for the male, and woman for his use to suck her energy, and drain her energy. He uses her erotic energy without responding to it, while not responding to her, nor making communion with her.

The Taoist view of Tantra is a little nicer, and tends to recognize the female energy as being healing for the male, rather than as causing the male to lose his energy to the female. The male interpretations of female sexuality are all distorted in one way or another, and in visual images such as the Tarot, they exploit the female for the good of the male, which is just another form of prostitution.

At the time I was researching the Tarot, I was also researching women's sacred images in the prehistoric. I researched the Paleolithic Venus figures found all over Europe, dating from the Stone Age *c.* 30,000 BC. I studied the wall art in European and Russian areas. I was also looking at different fertile valley cultures: the Indus Valley, the Sumerian Valley. I looked at the material concerning the early island of Crete, and the early island of Malta, the British Isles, the early Mayan and Mexican cultures, and the Peruvian cultures. I found that all of them have images of sacred women. I was constantly waking up through these images and cultures to the influence of the Divine Female.

At this point I began working with my friend Karen Vogel, and together we were drawing pictures of woman in matriarchal cultures. Karen and I together created a new feminist Tarot deck which we named Motherpeace.

All the work that I do now centers around the Motherpeace cards and my book. My teachings and my workshops integrate the images with yoga and the transforming healing work that I do.

I believe that for good or ill images are the most powerful force on the planet. I see how powerful movies and other visual images are in a negative way. I see how powerful television is, and we are deeply ingrained in cultural pictures through the media.

I think that images for healing – powerful, positive images like the Motherpeace images which were made in deep trance – transmit an energy that is very powerful. All one has to do is sit with them, look at them and they will change one.

I studied Rosen bodywork with Marion Rosen in Berkeley. My healing work, which is based on the Rosen method, and employs yoga and breathing methods, is very transformative. I feel that people can change almost anything that they want to – whether it's a tumor in their body, or whether it's a habitual response to reality, or a feeling of self-hate, or a lack of self-appreciation.

Bodywork talks directly to the body. It opens a deep wisdom. If one does bodywork over a period of time, one's essence eventually emerges. What one doesn't want to carry around can be let go of in a most organic, healthy way. One's essence emerges through the natural opening that occurs in good energy work.

My teaching focuses more and more on being authentic: being real. We should be who we really are here on this planet. I'm so tired of all the different spiritual cliches and programs that come out of our patriarchal society, telling us that the spirit is better than the body.

This mentality works towards dualism in whatever we do: "the spirit is better than the body so we should not be sexual; we should get to the point where we are really in touch with our spirituality, and we're really holy; where we're pure white light, and we don't need bodies, and don't have desires."

I think all of that is silly. I think we're here on the planet, and it's a most precious state to be in a body. We need to get *in* our bodies, instead of always trying to get *out* of them.

We need to stop abusing our bodies with all the chemicals and pollutants we put into them. The more in touch we can get with our bodies, the more in touch we get with nature and the earth, the happier and holier and more sacred we will be. The more in touch we become, the more spiritual, the more authentic, the more integrated our lives will be.

I find over and over again that my teaching involves looking at things as they really are, and trying to transmit a kind of clarity about what's happening. I say, "Yes, I really *am* a woman. I really *do* have a body. I really *am* a sexual being. My sexuality *is* holy. It is not cut off from the sacred. It has nothing to do with prostitution. It has nothing to do with commodities. It is not a commodity for men. It is a sacred experience that I hold in my body. It wakes me up to what is Divine and holy in the universe."

The Tantras say that "what is here is there. What is not here is nowhere." This is it. This is as sacred as it gets. Many have made a false splitting of life on earth. Life is not about the dualistic experience that many say it is within a patriarchal culture. I think women know this. There are studies which show that women are less loyal to civilization than men are, which I think is a very interesting comment on us women. Feminism as a spiritual path is awakening to what is real and what is authentic and what is truly spiritual.

I look at our culture and see that we're totally devoted to a patriarchal, death-oriented way of life. We basically come at it in the wrong way from the time that we come into this life, to the time that we go out of it. I look at the ways of our birthing and our dying. I see that we're so separated from ourselves, so separated from the sacred, holy way of coming into the world and going out: and both of these two events belong to the Goddess.

The ancient Goddess was the birth Goddess and the death Goddess. Fertility wisdom and shamanism are about crossing over between worlds. They are about birthing and dying.

If we can begin to bring our babies into the world with less pain, and less of a Judeo-Christian complex of believing that women should suffer in childbirth, we can get back to the sacred shamanistic experience of mediating between the worlds. The woman who brings a baby into the world is the quintessential shaman. She brings the soul from the "other side" to this side. She incarnates it. She forms it within her body and brings it out into the world, through her own bodily process.

Birthing is a spiritual experience. This culture has taken the sacred out of it. We take our birthing to the hospitals, which is about the least sacred, most sterile place in our whole culture. There are cold professionals servicing a woman's body there. They use drugs and chemicals rather than allowing her her own experience.

The central motif that changed when patriarchy took over from the early matriarchal cultures was that the birthing Mother Goddess was replaced by the mental Sky God who created the world through thought. We are at the culminating period for that metaphor. If we can take back our birthing, we can take back our Goddess.

The same is true for dying. We've got to stop going to the hospital to die. We've got to stop drugging ourselves with chemicals to go out, because going out is just going right back to the Mother. Dying is about going back into the light, back into Her arms. We go from the womb of this world into the womb of the other world. The sooner we understand that, and the sooner we have the courage to face death without chemicals and drugs, without escape, then the sooner we'll be home to our essential selves. And we'll be home to the birthing and dying experiences, and we'll be home to the Great Mother Goddess.

Profile 10

Starhawk

*Starhawk is a witch, and author of **The Spiral Dance** and **Dreaming the Dark**. She is a member of a collective called Reclaiming that gives workshops and classes, and puts out a newspaper on the Goddess religion and on public rituals. She is also a member of an affinity group that plans magic and rituals at political actions, e.g. Diablo Nuclear Plant and the Livermore Weapons Lab. She is currently teaching at Antioch West, San Francisco, and at the Institute for Culture and Creation Spirituality at Holy Names College in Oakland.*

I am a witch, and a witch is someone who practices the Old Religion, a religion we believe goes back to prehistory. It's the religion of the Goddess.

Witchcraft is a religion of ritual and it is a religion of magic practices. I like to use Dion Fortune's definition of magic as being "the art of changing consciousness at will." In that sense the whole basis of ritual and what we do is to create a transformative process.

I first got involved with witchcraft when I was a teenager. It was in the 1960s. I had found myself having a lot of powerful experiences in nature, and very powerful spiritual and mystical experiences that didn't seem to fall in the framework of Judaism – or at least not what I had been taught about it, or had learned about it.

I think, having grown up in Los Angeles, being out in any nature at all was like an amazing sensory shock. A natural environment is so much more complex than Los Angeles is. Just having a real clear knowledge that everything is alive and conscious. Later when I finally encountered some actual witches I felt their religion put a name on experience I had already had.

Magic is the practice of constantly working on a deepening awareness of the world around you. I've been practicing seriously and steadily now for nine years and there's a constant deepening. Sometimes it goes in spurts. I live in San Francisco. In the city I'm doing all sorts of things with my life, involving things like going to the bank, keeping records for the IRS! A lot of all those day-to-day detailed things, which is not like living off in a village, gathering the herbs. It's really very rare that I have any long stretch of time to devote purely to developing magic. There was one period of my life about nine years ago when I first moved to San Francisco. I did spend a lot of time just on magical development, and it was very, very important. It was crucial. It sort of got me over the first hump of having any kind of ability at all. Since then it's been really a juggling act. To me that is part of being a witch – not being someone who's removed from the world.

In religion what we call the Goddess, Spirit, *is* the world, manifested in the world, immanent in the world. The religion involves being part of the world, and that means trying to balance the development of a magical consciousness with living in the world today, which is a very, very different world from 7,000 BC or 35,000 BC. A couple of years ago I took a group of people to Ireland for almost three weeks to learn magic and to do ritual at a lot of the old sites. Having three weeks for me to just concentrate on magic, and the affect of the sites themselves – the places, the standing stones, and all the old sites – was very, very powerful. It opened up another dimension, another level. But now it's a constant growing process, and a constant changing. A lot of it, I think, is very gradual. There are things I can do now which I certainly couldn't do nine years ago, especially moving energy, and being able to channel and focus the energy of a group of people, even a large group of people.

Four to six years ago, when *The Spiral Dance* came out, we did a ritual for Halloween, partly as a celebration, and partly to do a really big ritual. We were worried how to do a ritual for four to five hundred people. We created this elaborate thing which was very wonderful, beautiful, and theatrical. Looking back on it I realize we gave so much thought to the difficulty of doing a ritual with that many people. Now when I travel or when I speak I like to talk and then do a ritual, and there usually are two to three hundred people there. It just seems very natural and easy now to do very simple ritual with that many people, and it works. The energy moves. It's directed gently, but leaves room for spontaneity. That amount of energy is no longer frightening to me, or no longer seems like something difficult. It seems very natural.

Actually a lot of that has come from doing direct action, ritual in jail and in situations where there are lots and lots of people. I was just re-reading some of the journals that I kept nine years ago when I was first beginning to lead group rituals, and some of it is almost sad – or you almost want to wince – when you read my struggles to feel comfortable with even a small group of people. There was this bouncing back and forth between not taking any responsibility at all, wanting it to be totally collective and leaderless, and then taking over completely and wanting to direct every single little part of it.

It's very hard to find a balance. I think it's hard for women in this culture too because we don't have many models of sane leadership. We certainly have even fewer models of women who have any power *with* other people as opposed to *over* other people.

It took me a lot of psychotherapy actually to learn to separate and draw the boundaries more clearly, and not feel like I had to take on rescuing the entire world. I think I always had the desire to heal, but it grew when I found an increased ability to heal and also an increased awareness of what my limitations are. That comes from witchcraft. It also comes from when I decided to go to school so I could combine practicing therapy with witchcraft. Of course I went in thinking I already knew more than anybody else about it. I just needed the stamp of approval. But I actually learned an enormous amount from going to school. One of the things I learned was how to step back and how not to totally take on what was going on with other people.

It also taught me about the limitations of working with other people. There's a vast difference between someone being helped and someone becoming empowered. You can't empower somebody else. You can set up conditions in which they can hopefully become empowered themselves. But if you're helping somebody else, you're probably disempowering them. There are times when everyone needs a little help, but it's a real delicate balance.

Back in the 1960s there was a group of anarchists in France called the Situationists. One of their slogans was "create situations." They were part of the uprising in 1968. Their idea is, if you want things to change you create situations in which people will have to confront certain things, and change. That's sort of how I approach therapy. What I do is create a situation in which someone can change. In some ways just having a place where you can talk to somebody about what's going on with you without being judged, where it's a really safe place, is a situation in which you can change. You can grow to accept yourself. Sometimes I use magic and ritual in the work. One client, who is a musician, would sit down to practice her instrument and she'd see her mother's face, and hear her mother's voice saying, "You'll never get anywhere. You'll never do anything. You'll never be any good." In therapy I had her draw a picture of her mother and we worked with my playing her mother and her having to fight me. She felt a great need for shielding, so I had her draw a shield for herself. I had her go home and put the picture up and put the shield on whenever she wanted to practice.

I also do a lot of trance work with clients because that way they can encounter aspects of the personality that are much deeper than what they encounter on the verbal level.

I usually have people lie down and do some kind of induction to take them to a place that we call a place of power. They look into the four directions to establish a base for themselves, in that world, and to establish a circle of protection. They see what their place of power is like, and from there they may go off and explore the different directions and encounter different beings or different symbols of parts of themselves.

I always thought being a witch is political in the broad sense. But over the past three or four years the people I work with magically have gotten very much involved with doing more direct political action. They are especially involved in environmental issues, in anti-nuclear work, anti-weapons work, anti-intervention, and in Native American support work. That's involved a lot of civil disobedience at different places. We've been involved with actions at the Diablo Nuclear Plant, and at Livermore Weapons Lab, and at Vanderburg Air Force Base. I also am a non-violence preparer. I do trainings for people to participate in actions that have involved work with a lot of other community groups. Everyone goes through a training before an actual action, and I also go to a training group for trainers. Our affinity group is called Matrix. We do magic and ritual together, and go to an action with an idea of doing ritual there. We see if it can be a focus, and if it's needed. We do our own magical preparations for an action.

I think that ultimately the effect of the kind of bridging of spirituality and politics is something that is very, very long range. I think we're very effective in planting the seeds. When I go around the country speaking or doing workshops, I feel the people are really hungry for the information, and hungry for the experience. Lots of people all over are taking my books like *The Spiral Dance* and using them to start their own circles and experiment and explore. When we go someplace like Livermore I think we're enormously effective in making people aware of the issue and focusing attention on it. We are showing an example of people actually doing something, taking some action. In terms of actually stopping the work of the weapons lab, the effect is small for the moment. Maybe we can shut it down for a day. We're far from being able to shut it down permanently because to do that would mean being able to change the entire system that supports it. But in terms of the consciousness of the people that work in the labs at Livermore, and people like the guards and police that work there, I think we are very effective.

The public relations director quit his job and began doing anti-nuclear work. The morale inside the labs has been very, very low and people are very distressed by the weapons work that goes on there.

People seeing other people taking action, like going to jail, affects them on a much deeper emotional level than just leaflets. Also in a way I think that it is a magical act in that it changes the underlying fabric, the sort of psychic structure surrounding the labs.

For me Judaism ties in with my political and spiritual work because it's my background, my blood, my culture that I was raised in. I'm sure there's a lot of aspects of my work that are very Jewish in a real gut-level and intuitive way. Especially the idea of the spiritual and the political. The spirituality not being removed from the world, but being part of the world, lived in the world. I had a lot of background in Judaism, and a Jewish education. I went through Jewish Bat Mitzvah, and later went to Hebrew high school, and also to the University of Judaism. I know all that has a strong influence on me. The Jewish influence comes more, I think, from the regular Jewish tradition, not just from pre-patriarchal roots. By the time you go back to the pre-patriarchal roots of Judaism, what you've got is basically witchcraft, or paganism. If you're throwing out four or five thousand years of the tradition and the history, you're not dealing with Judaism in an honest sense.

I had an experience recently where I was invited to be on a panel with another Jewish feminist, Judith Plaskow, and to speak to Bryn Mawr, and at the Reconstructionist Rabbinical College. It was very moving for me. I talked to them about why I had decided to move outside the tradition. I felt like there was an enormous amount of warmth and support from the people I was talking to.

I told my mother about it. My mother went off on this thing about wouldn't it be nice if I decided to become a reconstructionist rabbi?! It is so much more respectable than being a witch. Then she wrote me this letter saying that she had ridden down to a conference with a woman rabbi in Los Angeles where she lives. All the way down she was telling her about her daughter – her daughter's speaking, and writing, and this and that. Finally at the very end she mentioned my name – Starhawk. She said the woman nearly wrecked the car and said, "Your daughter is *Starhawk*?! Why didn't you tell me that before?!" She said, "I've got a piece of advice for you. Why don't you leave her alone? She's making a great contribution to

Judaism, right where she is." So my mother wrote me that. It was very gratifying!

But I think that's very true both for Judaism and other traditions. There's a lot of change going on within them. A lot of it has been sparked and a lot of it has been challenged by women who have moved outside of the tradition.

Profile 11

J. Ruth Strock

Ruth Strock is the founder and director of the Color Research Institute in San Francisco, a networking center for color research, designers, fashion consultants, and healers. At the center Ruth teaches Living Color Workshops, and a New Age Color Consulting Training. She also practices privately as a color consultant, and as a psychological counselor through the Transpersonal Counseling Center in Oakland.

My interest in color began as a child when I got my first set of oil paints. I admired the swirls of color that Van Gogh had intensely painted. Vision was my strongest sensory modality. Parents would say, "What big eyes you have!" and I would answer, "The better to see you with." My idealistic thoughts centered around the creation of beauty and form. The birth defect that I had in my left hand kept me separate from other children, yet I was genuinely happy and appreciative of Mother Nature. I sat for many hours staring up at the sky, or watching water-lilies on a lake. My painting continued at an Art High School in New York, where I met my first teachers of color.

At the same time I discovered Hindu masters who spoke of color and sound. Around the time of my parents' divorce I was reading books on Zen and taking classes which included guided imagery. I was experiencing a cultural paradigm shift from the mainstream of American society. Much of my generation reinforced this shift. The mass cultural interest in Eastern philosophies was exemplified by our heroes, such as George Harrison and Ram Dass.

By the late 1960s my mother and I moved to Greenwich Village in New York City. I had a yoga teacher whose inaccessible thoughts and feelings were of constant intrigue to me. I found myself adopting what seemed to be his world-view. I saturated myself with teachers of Eastern philosophies, in which self-effacement was encouraged. I practiced yoga sincerely, sleeping on a high board and waking up every morning at sunrise to meditate. I dreamed of living in a cave and serving an ultimate master in India.

I then journeyed with a Tantric artist and his family to California. I observed him drawing a *yantra* (an ancient image) every morning to center himself. He spoke of the physiological effects of putting water or mustard seed oil in different colored jars in the sun. He said this would solarize the water for healing purposes. My practices of yoga austerities grew. I went for seven nights without sleep and six months without speaking. I woke up at the holy hour of dawn to jump in a cold stream and incant Sanskrit prayers while burning incense made from cow dung and camphor.

I helped take care of the teacher's three children, and aided his wife in cooking. I made many pots of *chai* (Indian tea) while my teacher smoked the holy herb of Shiva that I had rolled into a perfect joint. He taught me Hindu wash painting, which is a form of oriental painting similar to painting by numbers, in that each color has a specific place to go, fitting neatly within the lines. It was lacking in free expression.

Later I went through a series of very painful internal experiences where I became very disoriented and frightened. I experienced a dissolution of self. At one point I looked in the mirror and saw many other faces. I went through a very lonely, confused period in which I had many psychic experiences where I felt out of control. As I surfaced from the dark voyage I began reintegrating my life and for a while turned away from the inner world.

In 1976, after returning from a summer vacation in Europe which fell a little short of the trip to India I had intended, I married a man from Iran. Together we plowed through the course work at a Northern California University. He was as pulled to the materialism of the West as I was to his ancient past. During the coup in Iran I was a refuge for him. Our religious commonality was in the rituals of the Jewish tradition. We lit candles on Friday nights and led sabbath services in our small college community.

In the marriage my costumes changed from hippie clothes, long dresses and unshaven legs to nylons, make-up and coifed hair. I felt the glamour and comfort of silk dresses, high heels and mascara. I began to become more conscious of beauty and harmony in my appearance.

Letting go of the religious Hindu conditioning, I rediscovered my sexuality. I submerged myself in my sensuality, which had long been suppressed.

There was a turning-point in the marriage where I felt a pull back to my spirituality, which I had kept solitary. In disdain I left him, projecting the limitations of the materialistic world-view onto him.

I took this newly-found sensuality, beauty, and education to explore what seemed like a new world. I landed in San Francisco, managing fashionable retail clothing stores. One morning on the radio I heard a color consultant speaking about the healing effects of color. Fascinated, I called the color consultant the next morning and asked her if she would train me in this new field. Three months later I began a course in training to be a color consultant.

I began my practice right away, integrating my intuition, my past knowledge of color, and the training. This work allowed me to become authentic and expressive. I spoke my inner truth in living color.

I created a class which is a ritual experience of the effects of color on the body, mind and spirit.

In my Living Color Workshop we talked about issues like: how we feel when we walk into a restaurant with a low-burning red candle at each table. What kinds of attitudes do we have about the tall woman who just walked in wearing a slinky, scarlet dress? What do we feel like doing when we come into a schoolroom freshly painted yellow? What happens inside our bodies when we slide into a blue car with a blue interior, and find ourselves entirely surrounded by colors of the sea and sky? If we close our eyes and envision ourselves in a deep, emerald-green rain forest, moist and abundant, and find a jeweled chest, what gift is waiting for us inside?

The focus of my work with color is not to answer these

questions for each individual, but to create a container for the intuitive mind to receive. I want each person to access his or her own channel.

People come to the Living Color Workshop who are willing to risk an acceleration in their own growth and are strong enough to choose to leave at any time if the colors are not serving them.

I create a colored environment each week where students are guided on a "rainbow" tour. Each week we focus on a different color ray of refracted light. The first week we start with all the tones and shades of red, such as rose and scarlet. The second week we experience orange and shades of brown and peach, then yellow, beige, and gold. We continue during the course with green, blue, indigo and violet. The course is eight weeks.

Initially I guided a small group in imagery concentrating on the color-of-the-week, and then lectured on the psychological effects of color. It seemed that everyone had something different to say about each color. One color therapist guarded against the mal-effects of red; others would say that red stood for strength and courage. All the material on colors seemed contradictory. At this point I gave up trying to know all the answers to the effects of color and decided to create a colorful experience.

On green week during a class series I brought lime jello from the back of my refrigerator. We had so much fun eating green food that I decided to include food in the course. Each week the class would come to my San Francisco apartment. I stripped the living-room of all furniture. I covered the walls with banners and placed objects throughout the room that were the color of the week. During blue week I set out blue bottles, blue irises, and blue books. With the room lit by a blue color therapy lamp, I guided the class in blue imagery.

The images came naturally and the pictures became clearer over time. Thought follows energy and energy follows thought. As people in the class thought themselves surrounded by blue in their mind's eye, they were indeed surrounded by blue. I created a sensual experience by tasting the color imagery, by serving blueberries and yogurt on blue plates. I included three books on the course, one on color psychology, one on color imagery, and one on women's transformation. I also wrote a workbook that guided the group through an inner searching process, and allowed them to contact the very ancient part of themselves: the part that knows everything they need to know about color.

Color ties in very closely with one's moods and emotions. It can remind us of early childhood memories – when we first saw red as a baby, or past-life pictures of ourselves in battle. The color experience magnifies our life experience. On red week some students expressed their anger at work. Others began exercise programs. We tracked our dreams each class to observe the unconscious material that was appearing with each color. Red week was a week of passion, heat, and sleepless nights. I observed many fears of loss of security or loss of a loved one.

The color course brought together artists who were stuck in their work, jewelers who wanted to more fully understand the significance of color gems, psychology students, interior designers interested in healing environments, kabbalistic magicians, hair designers, fashion consultants, body workers, and healers. I experienced joy at having found an expression of my true life-work, which is empowering and authentic.

People in the color classes asked me to teach a color consulting course. The course began as a vehicle to train people to become color consultants. One part of the course was specifically for training. The other half was for those interested in the healing properties of color. The experiential class grew to become the central focus of my work.

In my color consultations I was giving the students their colors and came to realize that they often came to me at a very vulnerable period in their lives. They were uncertain about their image and inner beauty. I realized that I was unable to serve them past the few consultation sessions. I wanted to fully be an instrument for their growth. I discovered a graduate school of transpersonal psychology which includes a focus on individual spiritual crises and spiritual development. Color was still the primary force which created a container for my talents, but my focus became personal evolutionary development. I became more aware of the importance for each individual to

access their own understanding of color. I became sensitive also
to the fact that I was merging with others. I was often doing it
unconsciously. I would feel myself slide into another's shoes.

Feeling my boundaries, and creating a circle of colored light
around me for psychic protection, became crucial. I worked
with the color class in grounding the group's light to the center
of the earth, and healing psychic wounds and scars with light
and imagery.

Images of color and light emerged for healing the planet. We
envisioned a green pyramid in the center of the third chakra in
our solar plexus, becoming smaller and smaller until it was
almost cellular. Then I asked the class to expand the pyramid to
include each of themselves, then all of us in the room, then the
block we were on, the neighborhood, San Francisco, the Bay
Area, Northern California, the United States, and then the
whole planet until the earth was resting gently in the healing
force of the green pyramid. We then reversed the process and
returned the emerald pyramid to ourselves.

My work in transpersonal psychology allowed me to heal
the split that had emerged within myself in my embrace of
Eastern and Western philosophies. My psychic and spiritual life
had become very private and singular up until the time when it
resurfaced in the course of my color work.

I became aware of the importance of color in the counseling
sessions, from the color of the walls in the counseling room,
to the color a client sees when they close their eyes. I noticed
that when therapists wear solid light colors, the colors reflect
more of the clients' material. The clients' colors are a major
factor in determining their psychological states. If the client is
wearing a lot of blue, I could safely make the assumption that
she or he is in an introverted stage focusing mainly on areas of
communication. If the client is wearing a lot of red, he or she is
probably in an extroverted stage, coming out more and
creating new attachments.

In my practice as a color analyst I have incorporated various
methods to help me select the appropriate colors for my client.
Early in my consultant practice I held two to three hundred
swatches up to a client and intuitively determined which ones
looked best on her. I would come up with twenty-five to

thirty-five colors for each person. Then the work evolved of its own accord. I decided to see the client in two sessions. One session served to take information in and the other to present the client with his or her colors.

I found unique methods of assessment to use in the first session. I had the clients sit down, close their eyes, ground themselves, and then imagine a flower at the top of their heads which they imagined filled with color. This gave me a clue as to the colors they were seeing inside. Some people would see an open, red chrysanthemum. Others would see a tightly-closed tulip. I had them draw the flower as a child would on a large sheet of paper with big crayons.

I then did the actual color analysis while asking them about their favorite colors and personal color history. I did a Tarot reading, selecting seven cards for the seven chakras. I used the Egyptian deck, because the pictures were large and full of color symbolism.

I drew the first card and related it to their security issues, which are concerns that arise when the person is vibrating in the first chakra. The second card I associated with the second chakra, and the issues that are connected with sexuality and relationships. The third card I related to their personal power, and so on. At first I viewed the cards as a way to understand the clients' life issues, but then people began to tell me during the consultation that the Tarot card reading relayed information regarding something that had happened for them during the previous few weeks. I then acknowledged that the Tarot readings were bringing into focus my clients' recent past.

While doing color consultations I opened more clairvoyantly. I became aware that an individual has had many lives before this one and many different looks and ways of presenting him or herself. I created an ethnic look for the client from his or her past-life pictures. If I saw the client in a past life in Egypt I pulled together a fashion look with Egyptian lines and styles from that part of the world. I saw one client with a past life in France with French lace.

I divided the clients' colors into three categories: work, relationships, and friends. These categories changed with each individual. I asked each client what he or she felt was lacking within each of the three life areas. Some said that within their relationship they wanted more autonomy or more sensuality. At work some people wanted a raise in salary, more recognition, or better communication. In the friends area some people wanted more intimacy and bonding, others wanted more lightness and joy. The colors I selected for each person's need helped to enhance that area of the person's life.

Aside from the classes and consultations I have given, I have also been lecturing on the effects of color. Recently I gave a lecture at the Association of Artist-Therapists, discussing these new age concepts of color as tools for healing.

In my home recently I held an "open house and artists' network," drawing together all the women from the Living Color Course to sell their artistic wares for the holiday season. There was much light and joy for us that day.

Presently I am planning a video of the color experience; I am bringing more color psychic researchers together; and I am developing a correspondence course. In creating the Color Research Institute in San Francisco I am realizing my vision of teaching and networking new age color workers.

Profile 12

Sandy Ingerman

Sandy Ingerman, MA Counseling Psychology, is a shamanic counselor, and teaching associate for Michael Harner's Center for Shamanic Studies. She has a private practice in Santa Fe, New Mexico, in which she uses shamanic techniques and the Tarot. Sandy teaches classes on shamanism and the Tarot throughout the country.

Many years ago I prayed very hard to be a channel for the earth. I love the earth so much I wanted to help with anything that our mother needed. I feel the earth created human beings so that she could dance through them. Much of my motivation to work with people is to open them up to the love of the mother that is trying to come through and to teach them how to dance again.

There are many ways to work with people, and I try to find the way appropriate to the person I'm working with, honoring where that person is at in this point in his or her life. I use the Harner Method of Shamanic Counseling, and the Tarot for individual work. During the course of shamanic work I teach people to meet a guide or teacher who gives them direct information about their own questions and problems in their lives. It's a wonderful method for empowering someone because one learns how to get answers for oneself instead of needing to be dependent on one authority figure.

A shaman is a person who journeys outside of time and space to retrieve information. A shaman enters into an altered state of consciousness to go to different territories in non-ordinary reality, and to connect with guides and teachers to retrieve information.

So basically what I teach people to do is to become a shaman for themselves. The technique for getting a person into an altered state is a monotonous drumbeat. This technique continues to amaze me with each person I use it for. The information people are bringing back from their guides and teachers is astounding. It seems to me that the spirit world is close, right now, ready to give any information that is needed. People who meet their guides and embark on shamanic journeying seem to feel more control in their lives and feel so much lighter and contented. Coping with daily life becomes less stressful and more enjoyable.

I would like to give a sense of what a shamanic journey is like. One of the most important steps in doing a journey is having a focus, intention, a purpose. The more crucial your question is the easier it is to obtain information.

Before doing a journey I call in the spirits and the four directions for assistance by using my rattle. This is done by shaking the rattle to the sky, and to the earth four times each, starting in the east. I do this while turning clockwise in each direction.

Once I have called in the directions I dance my power animal. In the shamanic tradition it is believed that all people have power animals, or guardians. A power animal takes pity on a person at birth and agrees to protect this person. Power animals/guardians change every few years. If a new power animal/guardian does not take over then that person suffers from a lack of power and becomes seriously ill or depressed. Then a shaman needs to hunt in "non-ordinary reality" to retrieve a power animal/guardian for the person. One can have more than one power animal or guardian.

I dance my animal because I want to give it attention and let it know it is wanted so it doesn't leave me. I will not reveal the identity of my guardian here because that is seen as bragging about one's power. When you brag about power you lose it. The easiest way to get rid of an unwanted power animal or lose one you do want is to brag about it.

The method to dance my animal is to drum or rattle for a few moments and allow my animal to move through me. I do this until I feel a strong connection with my guardian.

Now I am ready to lie down and begin my journey. I use a

drumming tape to enter the shamanic state of consciousness since I am journeying alone. Journeying is done in the darkness so I put my arm over my eyes to block out the light. A piece of cloth can also be used to accomplish this.

I want to get my intention of the journey clear before I begin. My question is: "Is there any information that I can retrieve for the readers of this book that will be important for them to hear right now?" I always say to people that I will attempt to bring back information. Saying that I will *definitely* bring back information is bragging about power, so I always use the words "I will attempt to" or "I will try to help you."

I am now ready to journey. The drumbeat that I will be hearing is at a frequency of seven to fourteen cycles per second. This frequence has been said to be the vibration of the earth. By listening to the drumbeat I will be aligning myself with the earth's vibration.

There are three different territories to travel to in a non-ordinary reality. There is the Lowerworld, the Middleworld, and the Upperworld. There are many levels down in the Lowerworld and many levels up in the Upperworld. Power animals and teachers in human form live in both the Lower and Upperworlds. Some people always have the same teacher. I often meet with different teachers.

I then decide to ask my question to a teacher in the Upperworld. But first I want to go to the Lowerworld to connect with my power animal. When the drumming starts I go down my entrance into the Lowerworld which is a tree trunk in a lush forest area. I enter into my tunnel which leads me to the Lowerworld. My tunnel is earthy and cool. It's not very smooth but very jagged. Everyone has a different tunnel. I run down my tunnel and enter into the Lowerworld where my power animal is waiting for me. I again find myself in a forest surrounded by huge pine trees. There is a clearing and a fire going inside the circular clearing.

My power animal starts to run in circles around the fire picking up such speed that she creates a whirlwind of smoke that lifts me up into the air.I keep floating up. First, I leave the earth and float up in the darkness of space, until I hit a membrane that I gently break through, leading me into the

Upperworld. I find myself in a cloud city where there is a teacher sitting on a white stone bench waiting for me. The teacher I meet is very ethereal looking and dressed in a blue gown. I can barely tell if it is a man or a woman, and it seems to change back and forth between both.

I approach this teacher and ask: "Is there any information that I can retrieve for the readers of this book that would be important for them to hear at this time?"

I find myself extremely overwhelmed physically, emotionally, and spiritually by the love for this being. The teacher says to me that it is important for all of us to see the abundance that is around us right now, that which so many of us forget about. First of all, we should appreciate being in human bodies. Spirits floating around in the ethers don't have the pleasure of actually having physical forms to move, dance, and play. If we love our own spirits and souls, we should take care of our bodies, enjoy and treat them in a sacred way.

At that point my teacher takes me by the hand and we start flying over different places on the earth. What this teacher is showing me is the incredible home we inhabit here on earth. My teacher shows me the abundance that the earth provides. We look at the trees, flowers, rivers, lakes, animals, plants, beaches, oceans, mountains, the warm shining sun, etc. We oftentimes get so caught up in "survival" that we lose our awareness of the beauty and abundance that surrounds us.

My teacher tells me that we should step out of the little boxes we have built for ourselves physically, emotionally, and spiritually, and open up to all of our senses: sight, sound, smell, feelings, to really experience where we live.

We should also open up our hearts to the love and light that is trying to come through the Mother and the Father. There is an abundance of love and support for those of us who choose to take the journey down into the depths of our own hearts into our own beautiful light. The spirit world recognizes what a hard journey it can be and offers us a lot of support to tap into.

My teacher also talks about the use of quartz crystals. He/she says that quartz crystals are a way to bring light back into our own bodies. Because the way to use crystals varies with the person using them, and with the crystals themselves, I encourage anyone who decides to take this advice to do some reading on the use of crystals and how to cleanse them. Ask the crystal you use for its purpose, and how one should properly use it. The best teachers of how to use crystals are the crystals themselves.

My teacher and I float up to another level in the Upperworld which has been described by many as the "crystal city." I've never seen any life up here, but it is a brilliantly constructed city of quartz crystals. I enter into a building made of quartz crystals, and into one the crystals themselves. The colors – greens, blues, reds, yellows – are blindingly bright. I allow the colors and the light to permeate my body, and feel the tension in my body melt away.

I leave this crystal abode and start my descent into the Lowerworld. I thank my teacher for the information, and my teacher reminds me of the importance of keeping our hearts open: listening and seeing with our hearts. My teacher talks about trusting our own hearts and taking care of our bodies as well as the beautiful body of the earth that we inhabit.

I slowly float down to the fire circle from which I left the Lowerworld. I play with my power animal, and when there is a change in the drumbeat signaling me to return, I run back up my tunnel and out of my tree trunk onto the earth, then back into my room. I am left with the teacher's question of "How open have I truly been to abundance?"

My work with shamanism blends with my work with the earth. Much of shamanism is based on earth knowledge. The drum is often called the heartbeat of the earth. Drumming aligns a person to the vibration of the earth and allows people to awaken to what Mother Earth has to share with us.

My favorite tool, the Tarot, provides one with a symbolic map of where a person is in the present. The Tarot also points out what his or her gifts and challenges are, and what possibilities one is moving toward in the future.

I use the Tarot with people to show them what their inherent gifts are in this lifetime and what the challenges and obstacles are that they have chosen to break through.

Symbols speak to the unconscious. The symbolic work with

the Tarot starts to promote changes from the inside out, working on a very deep level.

I use the Tarot either for a one-time consultation with people, or I use the symbols on a regular basis to help people break through blocks and to encourage creativity. One of the processes that is symbolized on many of the Tarot cards is the marriage of dualities and oppositions. Working with the symbols helps us to tap deep inside ourselves to what these polarities are about; then we can start to bridge them on a conscious level.

I oftentimes do guided visualizations with people to talk to a symbol or a teacher in a card and find out what the lesson is that a person is being asked to learn. We also find out what the changes are, if any, that this card is asking a person to make in his or her life at this point in time.

The beauty for me in both the Tarot and shamanism is that they both show a person that they have choices. They have the choice to create a happy life, and they have the choice to break through obstacles that obstruct them. What people start to experience is that making choices and taking responsibility for one's life is not that hard, and is actually very freeing.

The main focus of my counseling work is on the issue of empowerment. For too long many people have felt like victims of society and have taken on belief-systems that don't always allow one to feel in control of one's life. Getting people in touch with their own personal power and the willingness to take responsibility for their lives is important.

When I use the word power I don't mean power over other people – I mean the power to create what is needed in one's personal life. The power to move from one's intuition and center and not from one's fear and negative belief-systems.

Empowerment is an especially important issue for women. Women receive invalidation for their gifts and powers. Women's intuition has been labelled "old wives tales." Women who get in touch with their personal power often have a hard time in this society. Many men take empowered women as a threat.

In order for people to get in touch with their personal power they must love themselves. So many of us carry the belief that we're bad and that we will misuse our power if we're in touch with it. Many of us were told as children that we were bad and we believed it. Now we carry that belief into our lives.

Many people honestly believe that they don't deserve to be happy. How can we learn to create happiness, balance, and peace within our lives if we don't feel we deserve it? It's impossible!

Many people have the cellular memory that goes back before this lifetime of misusing power, and of being punished for it. Many women have some unconscious or conscious memory that they were burned as witches. Fear and the feelings of not being okay come up again with these power issues.

If one truly can learn to love oneself totally, the good and the bad, one then has available incredible potential to create wonderful things for oneself and for others. When we can learn to truly love ourselves unconditionally, we can learn to love others unconditionally. If we can love ourselves unconditionally we will not misuse our power.

Balancing our male and female energies is also part of the empowerment process. Many women are afraid of getting in touch with their own male energy because they equate it with symptoms of patriarchy. Women see what power misuse, greed, and force have led to, and they believe this misuse of power is a result of male energy. My personal belief is that positive male energy is about right action. Right action is about taking the information we get from our intuition, from deep inside ourselves, and then acting on it in the physical world. Right action is about allowing action instead of forcing action.

I feel the biggest obstacle in my work has been owning my own power. I have so many memories from past lives of misusing power, and of getting punished for using power, and of being misunderstood for being a powerful woman, that I have found I often block myself in my own professional and personal work in this lifetime. The fear of misusing power again comes up, as well as, "Will I be accepted and understood by others as a powerful woman?"

The key to working through my fear of misusing power has

been that I have been working on getting my ego out of the way of my work, and letting my higher self, the earth, and the universe work through me.

One of things I learned from Don Jose, a Huichol shaman, was that the way "to see" is with the heart. Because a lot of my work is centered around opening people's hearts, I find shamanism to be a very valuable tool in facilitating this opening in myself and in others.

Profile 13

Susana Eger Valadez

*Susana Valadez, grassroots shaman, and social scientist, is the director of the Huichol Center for Cultural Survival and Traditional Arts in Oakland, California, and of the Huichol Traditional Art Archive in Mexico. She is a contributing author in **The Art of the Huichol Indians**, a collection of essays. Susana lives with her Huichol husband and children in Mexico.*

I was eighteen when I consumed peyote for the first time. It opened me to spaces that I had never imagined. Having the experience of being open in that way changed my life and destiny. I had an experience of instantaneous awareness like pulling back a curtain. It happened in the context of my own culture, in the "flower child" days before I lived with the Huichols. The realization I had wasn't the idea advocated by Timothy Leary: "turn on – tune in – drop out." It was "tune *in* – and *do* something about the problems of this world." So my transformation came about when I got the message to stop looking at all the problems, and stop thinking about how terrible everything was in the world, but instead to actually find solutions to those problems, and to try to implement them. If you were to categorize my power base, my shamanic skills, or what I'm all about, it's called being an "active problem solver" in this messed-up world. My realization was that it was necessary for me to use the powers that my cultural base provided. I decided to use the stepping-stones of my own culture to envision a healthy radiant world, and to use the powers of my everyday life to make it that way. Everyone's life-path is paved with stones that guide one towards illumination, toward becoming a master shaman or shamaness.

149

Living now among the Huichols, my husband and I attend peyote rituals. I don't always understand the Huichol rituals, but I still experience the peyote in a special way. The Huichols have a prescribed behaviour that has been passed down for centuries. They know what to expect and their visions are tailored to their expectations. But for me, it's a little like a two-year-old going to a Shakespearean play! Trying to understand what's going on one can appreciate the pageantry, the beauty, and the colors; but for one raised outside of the Huichol culture, one has no idea of what's *really* happening based on their structure.

In the context of taking peyote with them, I was able to have my own vision. I didn't have deer come and speak to me, or have any of the Huichols' experiences. But while they were dancing and playing their music, the dance steps transformed into heartbeats. It was as if I was in the heartbeat of humankind. What I heard and felt was a thump . . . thump . . . thump . . . . I became alarmed when I flashed on the fact that this heartbeat is going to stop: that people from *my* American culture were giving the heart of humankind a "heart attack."

That was an important vision and lesson for me. I translated that vision to mean that I should dedicate my life to using my potential in order to keep that heartbeat going. A person from my culture has multi-resources. My power is my resourcefulness. I know how to manage things and apply this ability to help lessen the blow of this terrible giant – this "coronary" that is devastating the Huichols.

My background is in anthropology. I got my Masters in Latin American studies, which was interdisciplinary. My emphasis was on psychology, anthropology, and ethnobotany. I was always interested in indigenous populations. The knowledge that they have kept in their cultures remains because of their strong connection to Mother Earth.

That knowledge was given to all human beings, somewhere back in time. This knowledge is still so vital and important to us and is the most important treasure in the world, though we may not remember its importance while we're driving down the freeway. What I'm basically after is saving the treasure for our children, using the old guidelines to revitalize our planet. I have a vision of what I should be doing in this life, and how the world should be. I have a goal even if it seems impossible to attain. I try to get as close to it as I can. Every day in my life I try to get a little closer to that goal.

My education gave me the competence to find small solutions to many of the world's problems. But the "school of life" has given me the skills to use my potential, and to be competent at what I do. Being out in the world and daring to follow my heart, I find I'm pretty much able to do what I need to do in this culture. Sometimes I can't even pay the rent, but to me that is not a measure of success. It's a lot different from the frame of thought of most people, because in this culture the measure of success is money. But my measure of success is how I survive day by day, and how I continue my work day to day, and how I get closer to my goal. As far as that goes I'm totally capable and competent, which is what I think is real power. To just get through life, and not be affected by the surrounding structure, but to create your own structure, that is what matters.

I'm old-fashioned. I still have the sentiment of the 1960s, that "love is the answer." I'm not into war, politics, or putting weapons in the heavens. I'm into love, compassion, and nurturance. My ticket in life has been to try and spread as much love as I can, because it is the only counter-balance of all the evil and negativity in this world. I can't say that I go around never getting mad, or never getting down on people, but I basically think that the medicine that humanity needs to get back on course is a huge dose of Mother Earth's bosom: nurturing love.

Love translates into work too, very mundane work. The work I do at the Huichol Center includes cleaning up bathrooms where people don't even know how to use the toilets; teaching women how to cook on gas stoves; taking Indians out of jail who shouldn't be in jail in the first place. The Indians come to work in a Mexican town where they are treated so poorly. They get sick and have problems. My husband and I run a center for the Indians, called the Huichol Center for Cultural Survival and Traditional Arts.

We're an Indian/American family. The marriage of Mariano

and I in our small town in Mexico (which incidently is outside of the Huichol homeland) is a statement of faith in humanity. It surprises the Mexicans that an American is married to an Indian. From our marriage the message communicates that "we're all flesh and blood." There are good people among us, and bad people among us, though we shouldn't concern ourselves with judging people. We should concern ourselves with getting to know that people are what they are, but when we can find a place for each other in our lives, and enjoy each other, that is better than judging. That's how my philosophy translates itself into my work. The goal of my work is to find the solutions for a people facing extermination, a people who need our help, and need to be appreciated. The Huichols come out of their homeland and they're looking for work. They used to be corn traders and they were able to trade a sack of beans for a horse. Now they need money: a cash economy to continue their traditional way of life. They need to pay cash to go on their religious pilgrimages, because their traditional trails have been blocked off by barbed wire. So they come to the coast to work in tobacco fields. In their own land they feel like kings and queens.

Even though they have barefoot kids, and sleep in blankets with holes in them, their measure of success is not wealth. Their measure of success is how one accomplishes one's goals and how one carries out one's visions. The Huichol people live simultaneously on many different levels of reality. The dream world, the god realm, and the visionary world are a dominant part of Huichol life.

Now their attention is shifted to survival in the modern world. When they come to Mexican society where they are forced to participate, they are treated terribly with no respect at all. The imminent danger is that the Mexicans are trying to force them to be Mexicans and not Indians. By introducing roads, and schools, and all these alternatives, they are almost forcing them to change their ideas about their own culture. The Huichols don't know how to say "no," because they've never had anything like this happen to them before. They have no idea of the outside world. My husband Mariano who has come and lived in the American culture goes back and tells his Huichol friends about things like the atomic bomb and the movie, *The Day After*. They are totally innocent of what the outside world is like. They have no idea of the destruction which lurks over them.

Over the last two decades the Mexican government has attempted to integrate the Huichols into the mainstream of Mexican life by building roads, schools, factories and airstrips in the Sierra. Now there is also a government effort to convert the Huichols from their age-old system of barter to a monetary economy. The Huichols depend on the outside world now more than ever before and a tremendous economic emergency has been created. Some Huichols have been able to sell their art work to meet their needs but since the market for Huichol art is still not developed enough to allow their economic self-sufficiency, many Huichols leave the Sierra to seek employment. Some never return: they die, kill themselves, turn to alcoholism, or deny their heritage under the influence of the modern world.

Mariano and I get the medical supplies, food, and shelter that people need. We try to keep the traditional arts alive by saving their own patterns in embroidery, weaving, and beadwork, as well as by archiving them.

One of the most rewarding aspects of my work with the Huichols is to see the results of my efforts to help them preserve their beautiful and fascinating culture. I feel so privileged to have entered into their lives at a point in history when their traditions and art styles are still strong, rather than coming in later and try to salvage what might have been left. I've had my work cut out for me in the last ten years. Not only have I been trying to record an incredible amount of cultural information, but at the same time I have tried to make the Huichols aware of the worth and importance of their great knowledge and tradition. I have tried to inspire them to hang on to it.

The Huichol Art Archive is one project that has progressed very nicely. It began eight years ago when I lived in the Huichol homeland and installed a small museum of traditional patterns in my adobe home. I took the patterns from embroidered traditional costumes, all of which reflect Huichol religion and cosmology, and are direct statements of the Huichol identity and world-view.

As Western influence is becoming more intrusive in their culture, traditional designs are disappearing, and the ethnic integrity of the Huichols is diminishing. Designs from the shamanic tradition of eagles, deer, peyote, and mystical animals are being replaced by cars, cowboys, and even Mickey Mouse! These new designs are easy for the Huichols to find in the needlepoint books they acquire from outside sources. The needlepoint books they buy in the markets take the place of traditional patterns, so I collect old patterns to offset this.

Since much of the Huichol art is inspired by very complex aspects of their peyote religion, and outside patterns are interfering with a traditional network of symbols and guideposts which function in the religious and educational process, it is an absolute priority to insure that the original patterns are not lost in the current Huichol move toward fashion. They try to be fashionable with cupids and valentines on their clothing.

The approach I've taken to this problem has been to document as many designs as possible and then to make those designs available to the Huichols. Designs have disappeared from some communities more than others depending on the rate of acculturation. So the archive serves as an essential clearing-house where lost designs can be rediscovered. I painstakingly collect the traditional patterns from many Huichol women, then graph them out on paper and photocopy them. Then they are distributed to the Huichols who come to the Center or on my trips to the Sierra. I love to see the reaction of the Huichols who come to the Center for the first time and see all the beautiful designs desplayed on the walls. It's dazzling! They now have a written record of their heritage, and designs they can select from and take home.

In addition to the embroidery, I've also collected hundreds of samples of beadwork and weaving which I make available to them in a lending library. Many Huichols come to the Center on weekends for the sole purpose of copying beadwork or weaving designs. This ensures that the designs still circulate in the culture and helps Huichol families to build an economic foundation based on the sale of artwork with original designs. At a time when the Huichols are being forced to leave their homeland, this project becomes a major advantage for Huichols who want to stay in their homeland and work at things they are skilled in and enjoy. There is a good chance for the Huichols to remain economically self-sufficient by producing high-quality art with authentic designs.

It's fulfilling for me to see people whose costumes were filled with "outside" designs now coming to the Center with traditional designs taken from our archive. Some Huichols bring me patterns lost and rediscovered from older relatives. They have brought many designs that I still haven't recorded.

The Huichols use art the way I think art was "originally intended": that is, to give form to the sacred, to take inner visions and transform them to the physical plane. Ritual and art both transform the sacred to the human level. Ritual and art are still alive and well in Huichol culture. That's what they have to teach us. Their cultural consciousness seems far more evolved than our own. They use art to better their lives and strengthen their ties with their Creator.

I have a notebook with pen drawings that show how the Huichols learn to become shamans. The pen drawings were done by a Huichol shaman whom I've known many years. He's one of the few people who understands what I'm trying to do and is completely committed to helping me.

He has chronicled in pen and ink all the different Huichol power objects, deities, ritual paraphernalia, and ceremonies. Exposure to and experience with these things are what the children start with from day one, until the day they become accomplished shamans. I have tapes in which my friend explains what every object is, their importance, and how they are used. The drawings are step-by-step maps of how the Huichols go about teaching their children in the Huichol way. They give me the Huichol interpretation of what is important to them. This provides a good foundation from which I can formulate creative questions. It has proven to me that in order to ask the right questions, one has to have the basis of that knowledge. One has to know how things fit together, so that revealing questions can pinpoint specific knowledge and practices.

Mariano's yarn paintings also record important details about Huichol culture. He elaborates on the details in his paintings, and I fill it in with words. It's a combined effort to get these important details recorded before they disappear into the surrounding Mexican culture.

Mariano's paintings are of magical plants and animals. Shamans will eat the hearts of the birds to learn their secrets. For the Huichols, it works, although I'm not sure it would for non-Huichols if we tried it. Belief is part of anybody's destiny, and a large part of the shamanic path.

If you believe that shamanism is your path, and that this method is supposed to give you a certain knowledge, or a certain capability, or a certain skill, or cure, or power – it sure as heck might. Belief is the blood of life. I could be a neuro-surgeon if I wanted to to. I believe I could do it because I know the steps to becoming one. The same is true for the Huichols. They can learn how to bring clouds for rain, or find lost objects, or cure people who have diseases, and how to travel into the spirit realm. They can learn those steps because it's been proven for them. They are "cultured" to become shamans.

Before I was an anthropology major I was an art major in college. Art was the vehicle I used to study the ancient cultures, human motives, and the human psyche. I learned a lot about humanity by studying the way people express themselves. Art is an expression and an appreciation of what one has inside. The study of art gave me a wonderful base to discover who I am. Now I'm a "transcultural mom," both to my own children, and to my "adopted" Huichol family. With my nuclear family, I live between many belief-systems and levels of being.

I'm a rebel. This is my protest. I live in Mexico trying to do some good. Every bowl of soup I serve up is one notch on my belt. One more point to counter the baby-killers: the people who destroy, who build the bombs and weapons to kill our babies. I'm a rebel because this is my way of fighting for life. I fight with love and nurturance, not hate. That's what I consider to be notches on my belt: communication and nurturance are the keys to peace and global problems.

Everyone can find out where one's powers are and make changes. My way is to help keep traditional peoples on this earth so that we can relearn all that we've lost. Let's walk into the twenty-first century with our Mother Earth and all of her beautiful peoples leading the way. Then we as humanity will make a giant leap forward.

Profile 14

Brooke Medicine Eagle

Brooke Medicine Eagle is an earth-keeper, a visionary, healer, teacher, poet, and singer-songwriter. Her concerts focus on "singing joy to the earth." Her groups journey into beautiful and sacred places which deepen contact with earth-sky, body, and spirit. Raised on the Crow Reservation in Montana, she draws from a rainbow blend of Native American teachings, Feldenkrais practice, Neurolinguistic Programming, and the Masters of Light. Her dedication is to the timeless laws of a fully human way of life which nurtures All Our Relations.

I was raised almost alone, with my brother, mom and dad, five miles from the nearest ranch, ten miles from the nearest reservation village, and fifty-five miles over dirt roads from any large town. My experience of wanting to heal came on its own. I didn't have any form given me, nor anyone paying me special attention, because we were all busy on the ranch. The desire to heal emerged out of my own experience.

Fortune has taken me back to native medicine people and to healers around the world, yet I still get the same basic message from them: "You will never be given a traditional form. The form that is yours is the formless form, which breaks through to Spirit." This is what has been given me. And while it may sometimes seem wonderful to have such freedom to choose, I have (especially in the cloudiest moments!) wished for an elder or teacher who would "make it easy for me" by saying, "This is the way. This is the tradition. This is how we've always done it. This is what's right." Yet that hasn't been present, and I do think Spirit has a good reason for everything. I'm now maturing into the realization that whatever path is mine,

159

however it's related to tradition, it is a *new* way. This is a new time on earth we're coming into; one of my challenges is to bring us gracefully over the rainbow bridge into a new age. The ancient ways are being held beautifully by people well trained in them since childhood, and while I also carry some of these, what I'm personally given to do is what we're all to do at our own level – to step into a pattern that we've never ever had before. We've never ever all had peace on earth. Never have we two-leggeds stepped consciously into the Great Circle of all things – of the wingeds, the four-leggeds, the rock people, the grasses, trees, waters, and all earth's children.

Through visions and dreams, I was given the name Medicine Eagle, which can be interpreted as Little-Sister-of-the-Eagle-who-walks-the-Medicine-Way, the way of wholeness and healing. This name calls one to fly high and see far, to the way of vision and prophecy, to carry messages and light of a new time strongly across the sky. That name is not just a name like Joe or Nancy – it is an assignment. As I look back I understand so much more than I did when the name first came. Flying high and seeing far, carrying messages across the land was a very accurate description of my life. My intention was and is to awaken us to a graceful and harmonious transition into a time of peace – manifesting the golden dream that each of us holds in our heart. So Medicine Eagle continues to unfold and manifest itself in more and more beautiful ways.

Now I've been given a new name by the Masters of Light, who are my inner guides – that name is Chaliśe (Shah leaśe) and means "a chalice overflowing with light." I've had enough experience to be clear that this, too, is an assignment, and a very different one. While the eagle energy for me was active, moving, flying, giving a lot of energy out, masculine in tone; Chaliśe is feminine, receptive, being filled and spilling over. My challenge is to truly become a chalice to receive and channel light. The coming years will reveal much more than I now consciously understand; yet I *do* know that I find myself living in one place for the first time in many years and folks are coming to me. I have a studio and a "meditation" tipi where I'm bringing the light in . . . into one place. One of my visions expressed that I am to create/build a pillar of light that holds up the sky. I'm being taught to bring that pillar of light down, to hold it steady and let it flow over and out to the far reaches of earth. I'm looking forward happily to seeing what that light brings to myself and others. I see that the intention of my spirit is enormous, and very powerful in my stillness; when I am at the center, there is no time or space.

I've been called and guided and confirmed by light, illumination, radiance. When I first met the woman who was to be my medicine teacher, she reached out and touched my hand, just a tiny, infirm, blind woman. And she transformed into a radiant woman of light who stood over me, bathing me in radiance from every part of her body. I didn't follow her form in a traditional way, but that was a transforming experience. It was obvious that a special connection of spirit had been made, and although she has passed beyond, we are still profoundly connected. She teaches me and is available to me even now.

Another instance was the first time I met one of the most respected Lakota elders. I walked into his home, basically unannounced. When he saw me from his chair, he opened his arms and sent an enormous shaft of radiance to bathe me, his face and being transforming into light. The humorous part is that it disturbed his wife, who gave him a sharp blow in the ribs with her elbow and caused him to jerk and withdraw it. I've always been curious about what would have transpired had that interruption not occurred!

Much shamanic experience describes going into the darkness and coming back. The great darkness that I face in my work is the murkiness and limited nature of most daily life – I sense that all of us are living right now in a time of darkness when we compare it with the radiant world that is coming to us. Awakening us out of the darkness and the death of limiting habits and patterns from moment to moment is a part of my work.

The source of light for me has also been internal. I know that there is a light in me that grows and grows, filling and healing me, and pouring over. It comes through the center of me from the Source of all things. If we can but open to it, that light lies in every situation and person. Those moments when it radiates powerfully are truly an awakening – like the power of the east on the Medicine Wheel: illumination and awareness, wakefulness and rebirth, springtime and the golden light of dawn. When that light calls me, I always respond.

Light and lightness have other meanings for me as well. Lightness means letting go of burdens, of excess weight. It can refer to "lightening up" the heaviness of a situation. I'm reminded of graffiti I once read: "Angels fly because they take themselves lightly." As we lighten up in all ways, we become less dense, more filled with Spirit. Earth and physical bodies are the densest experience our eternal spirit can have; our challenge is to fill and balance it with the lightness of Spirit. There is a whole new quality of light coming to help move us into a new time, and I think it affects us deeply.

I believe that one of my tasks in this world is to challenge straight lines and boundaries, to soften them into natural curving flow. For example, take your arm and hand out from your body as far as you can easily; then move it around, reaching gently up and down and forward and back and all around. What you'll find is that your movement is circular, curved. In order to draw a straight line in front of you, it is necessary to tense some muscles, to restrict the free curving which is natural. Do it with awareness so you can begin to feel in your body the difference between your unrestricted flowing motion and the selective restriction needed to draw a straight line. As you move in freer and larger circles, whirling even, you will understand with Black Elk that power resides in circles, in allowing circulation, in recognizing cycles and spirals in our lives and projects, in stepping into the power of oneness with the Great Circle of all things. The finest martial artists demonstrate for us that spinning and the circular energy of free-flowing movement of our body is where true power lies.

Another example comes from different kinds of living space. Summer living in a tipi is cool and fresh; the breeze comes in under the rolled up sides, spirals and moves continually upward, cleaning and clearing. A continuous circle of coolness is created. Yet in a modern straight-line house, the windows are up at a certain height, and, if you are lucky enough that they actually open, the circulation doesn't cool down to the floor level or in the corners. Straight lines create corners of dead energy, dead air and dust. There is a great difference in living in those two kinds of environments. I wonder what is the maginitude of the effect on my nervous system if I spend my times in those straight lines and trapped energy. I've been involved in building lately, creating six- and eight-sided solar buildings, with floor venting built in, attempting to work with the great circles of sun and air that the Great Spirit gave us.

Another aspect of straight lines and boundaries has become clear to me living in Oklahoma. I'm especially aware when I go for a ride on my horse that *at least* every mile there's a section line in the road, which means a fence. In many places there is a gate every five minutes. I'm understanding that, as we draw those lines and fence in other of earth's creatures, what we do is to fence *ourselves* in – stop ourselves from free movement. Our bodies are so literal that this is a powerful statement. If I walk outside and come immediately to a fence, that's an experience of my nervous system, which echoes through all my experience, creating a pattern of limitation. A beautifully different experience is created riding for twenty or thirty miles unrestricted on my home reservation in Montana.

Another aspect of straight lines and boundaries is language. English is a noun/thing oriented way of speaking, of patterning our nervous system. If you're a Catholic, or a lawyer, or a dog, or a tree, there is a solid, limiting definition, a square box into which it fits. Many Indian languages, however, are very different. I'm slowly learning the language I was never given as a child, and when I first asked the old ones something simple like, "How do you say buffalo?" they would look at me really funny. They would have to ask, "What kind of buffalo, how many, what are they doing, what kind of day is it . . . ?" There is a tiny "root" for buffalo, but each separate situation is built into the word that is used for it. Buffalo is a process, a continually moving creation, not a thing. Their language is a moving, process language. And I know that such languages are very important to us; they set up a structure in our nervous system for a much more flowing and harmonious and alive way of relating to our world. It saddens me that even many full-blood children are not being given their native language.

My hope is for preserving and expanding that kind of language pattern.

In another incident, I was given a profound teaching about the way of living that is so important as our lives change more and more rapidly – about shamanic balance. Most of us think of life as a path, the best being the straight and narrow, where we can plod along without change. I think life is more like flying a glider. A fine pilot was giving me a demonstration ride, sitting directly behind me in this sleek, exquisite bird of a soaring ship. He had a stick for guiding it which connected directly with the one in front of me. I had my hand gently on the stick to get the feel of his controlling the plane. It wiggled a little bit, here and there, but basically seemed to be held in the center, as far as I could tell. Sensing that I was loving the experience and very comfortable as a "big bird," he offered to let me fly and I accepted, holding the stick tight and steady. Well . . . the wind caught us immediately and practically flipped us over! he said, "Would you like to try that again? Controlling it, holding it solid doesn't do the trick. You've got to feel that wind with that stick. Be like a bird, constantly moving and changing its feathers to catch the wind and glide. It seems subtle when I'm doing it – a constant sensing and playing the wind." So I tried again, and I could feel what he meant. It was never a straight line, never solid, tight or set in strong. It required continuing awareness and wakefulness and sensing in my body, connecting itself through the glider to the wind and to the rest of the world. This is such an elegant metaphor for the path that is mine and yours and the shaman's – changing with the breeze, moving like water. If we hold tight to a form, any form, I think we lose it.

The more I understand of neurophysiology and other healing ways, including that of Moshe Feldenkrais (the Israeli movement awareness genius), the clearer I am that my work is about finding ways to help us move as shamans always have: to challenge the darkness; to awaken ourselves by breaking through daily habitual form into Spirit; to awaken again and again and again; to open space in all our "knowns" for the incredible, awesome unknown. Teachers and elders through the ages remind us that we do, in fact, fall asleep. We do fall into habit; that's our very nature. The neurological studies show us that whatever we do, we form patterns, and if there are no patterns inherent, we find a way to make patterns out of the unknown that make sense to us, that fit what we know. We two-leggeds are constantly putting form on things, patterning them and forming habits. And habits are wonderfully useful; as we learn and put actions on automatic we don't have to pay so much attention to each little thing, opening the way for new learning. On the other hand, daily habit and what has been done in the past – what we did yesterday and what the way was fifty years ago, and on and on – are forms. We can draw intelligently from these forms; yet we must not forget the other side – the absolutely formless which has never been limited. Inevitably, as we bring the formless into our consciousness our human nervous system will form it and limit it. The challenge is to play on the edge – the edge of the unformed. Part of the shaman's way is that exquisite balance – between light and dark, in and out, left and right, formless and formed. So my work is to awaken myself and others so that we can joyfully play that line, that very fine line. It's not like a solid, straight path through the woods, not anything like that. It's a line that moves through bodily experience, with no form or pattern that you can name. A shaman's way is to keep moving along that line and continually reminding others, helping others along the distinct pathway which is theirs alone.

As I work with individuals and groups, I focus a lot of attention on their bodies: to bring a kind of fluidity and openness, grace and possibility to bodies that are stiff and bent, restricted and scowling; to move through the strictures that have developed over time; to break through habits and the daily form of things; to move through who-people-think-themselves-to-be and to touch the absolute grace and elegance which Spirit gifted each one. I use movement work which creates awareness. It's very fine and detailed work that brings people into wakefulness, that embodies their spirit and aliveness. I live on beautiful, open land, so I have the opportunity to get people out on Mother Earth and moving. A combination of such things helps awaken people.

There's another way I'm working with the body. On the

ranch we have a high-challenge ropes course. It consists of ropes and wires and logs in various combinations from three to fifty-five feet in the air. Folks are hooked into a safety system, and thus have the opportunity to play with their balance at some pretty high levels. When I learned, in years past, it was not so "safe," I began simply standing on a rock or log on the ground, then onto one foot, then onto something higher and higher and higher and smaller and smaller. The thrill is to balance on tiptoe atop the highest precipice, arms outstretched as though flying, one leg extended straight behind like tail feathers, to literally dance there. This practice teaches a kind of balance. And it's very useful because once we have balance in our body and nervous system, we use it at every level of our life. If from any place we stand, we have the choice to move freely and gracefully in every direction – backwards, forwards, sideways, up or down – we also then have that freedom in our daily experience, in the challenges we meet every day.

On the ropes course folks are safely harnessed, and hooked in; there is no danger. At the end of one thirty-foot-in-the-air-series of wires and balance logs, they climb to a 55-foot platform from which they jump into open air (riding a zip line 500 feet out and down). They leap into the unknown *literally*. Some wonderful patterns can be wired into the nervous system under this kind of intensity. Even though their mind knows they are safe, often they experience great fear. We stand on that tiny platform as I get them ready, and we both get to observe *fear* – to watch its play. What I'm talking with them about is that whatever they do in this intense situation sets a strong pattern, cuts a deep groove in the nervous system. They have a powerful opportunity for courage or for freezing up. So I say, "Step up here now that you're ready. Take a nice deep breath. Set a pattern of absolutely going for it, leaping through the fear into the unknown with the understanding that everything is going to be fine." And when folks understand that they are creating a pattern of how they breathe under pressure, a pattern for their willingness to step with courage into the unknown, for dealing with fear, then they "go for it." It may take them a few moments, but they go for it. That zip down the line, flying free, is exhilarating and incredibly fun. Paul Simon said in a song, "You need to learn how to fall before you learn how to fly!"

This kind of pattern is important to people in our modern time when so much unknown comes at each of us so fast. I was given a teaching once through my inner guides, when I was concerned and confused about where I was going and what was right. I was unsure. The message was this: "What you need to be sure of is that *every* step you take now will be a step *off* the cliff, into the unknown. When you lift that foot, there will be nothing under it. Yet when it comes down, it will be on the ground, on new ground. ALL YOU HAVE TO DO IS KEEP STEPPING!"

My stories are metaphors for the fact that all before us is new. We haven't done it before. There is no known pattern. There is nothing under our feet. I see that for *all* of us. Something I can do, as well as modelling that courage in my own behavior, is to make it all right for others; getting them to understand that they *can* leap joyfully into the unknown. That's all there is anyway, so they might as well approach it with their eyes open, alert, curious, breathing fully. As for security/safety, all we have ever had (talking about shamans challenging the darkness) and all we have now is our awareness, our wakefulness, our fullness of spirit in this body. We use the snakes on our ranch to teach folks. Instead of making safe little paths and killing the poisonous snakes, we say to the campers, "Snake people live here; this is their home. You're coming into their home space. The only thing you need do is to be in good relationship with them, and part of that is paying attention to where your big feet are. PAY ATTENTION! Be aware of what you're doing; stay in the present. Be wakeful. Know that creatures live here. Know that the grass is alive. Know these things when you take each step. And if you are awake and aware and present, you may get a little start, but you're never going to be hurt."

A story comes to mind of Jan who was terrified of snakes. She would always try to go by mowed paths and make sure her tent was on one. Mid-week we were playing a game called "Coup." We were playing at the dark of the moon, in two miles of unknown territory, pitch black. Each team was crossing the opposite way, hoping to find and "count coups" on the other. Jan got so excited and so intent upon her game that she crawled on her belly over much of the territory in the dark. Afterwards she spoke about it. When we asked her if she ever thought about snakes that night, she replied that her experience was much bigger than snakes. We had created a state of excitement, interest, intensity and newness against which the old fear of snakes could not compete. After that night she simply walked through the grass paying attention.

The energy that I'm giving out is moving concentric circles outward. I'm on an inner process level now – learning and taking the next step for myself. And all the while, my intention is to serve the whole. The intention of my spirit is immense. I work for Mother Earth and all her children, reminding the world again and again of the feminine: that the highest principle is to nurture and take care of one another. All things will follow from that. The sacred lodge where I have been taught symbolizes this feminine, nurturing, renewing energy, and in my own way I carry that message into the world.

To simply be and to have strong, unbending intent is a characteristic of the feminine, a very powerful one that most of us have forgotten. As I stay in one place, walk the land, commune with trees and wind, weave, and make clay pottery, an old part of myself worries that I'm not doing enough. But my deeper self understands that I stand powerfully beneath earth and sky, weaving a hoop dream of harmonious life on earth; that my intent toward that joyful time is unbending; and that it is very powerful. It's the same with my intent for all fences and boundaries to come down. I'm not out tearing down fences, yet because my intention is unbending and strong, everything I do contributes in some way to that happening. My work right now is an inner work that extends through my center to Source and thus to center of All-That-Is. And that's where change comes about anyway.

So my challenge now is as a model of that kind of intent. I touch the lives of many individuals who come to me. As each one of them transforms, they shine the light of that inner attainment and make a difference in their world. The focus of my work with each person is to find and grow and give forth the unique spirit gift that only they can give, thus doing the highest service to all. Another aspect of it is to hook them into the larger circle, because unless we all wake up to such facts as we are draining water under the Earth at an unprecedented rate – that our children are endangered by this – then our own excellence is pretty shallow. We all must wake up to the larger life around us. Healing the circle within ourselves may be the beginning, and then to heal the circle of our family, our community, our land, our entire human family, and all our relatives on Mother Earth. The patterns I hope to stimulate and set are the ones our native elders have long understood and practiced: (1) develop and express your unique spirit gift (2) in service of *all* your relations. When we can truly experience that we are one with each other and all things, then the transformation will be complete, the sacred pipe will be in and of our hearts.

PART III
THE NEW SHAMANIC
COMMUNITY

FERTILE CHANT

Shaman woman . . . dance
passion rise . . .   drip
shaman man . . .   come
fertile seeds . . .   grow

tree spirit
moon spirit
sun and rain goddesses
bless my womb
bless my lover's virility
we have suns to grow
and moons to reap

rain
come
quench
this fertile cry
           drench
           this song
until it is   wet
and new   born.

Chapter 1

The need for shamans

As women uncover their primal power and sacred roots, they also uncover the primal power and spiritual heritage of men, which predates militaristic traditions. In *c.* 7,000 BC, Old Europe, and in *c.* 3,000 BC, pre-India, women and men practiced a spiritual technology together, which has come to be known as Tantra. Tantra means to yoke together.[1]

Tantra is a system of beliefs and practices that utilizes the body's magic and power. "To yoke together" refers to the practices within Tantra wherein the vital forces of the body are released and then consciously united within the body. The worship of *sakti*, or female energy, is meditated on in conjunction with male energy. Tantric adepts teach that there are two currents that run parallel along the spine, one male and the other female. Through contemplative exercises the initiate can raise the kundalini, which contains these two channels, up the spine to the crown of the head where the two energies meet. Metaphorically, the meeting of the two energies can be viewed as a consummation of life currents, or a conjugal union. When an inner consummation is achieved, the Tantric practitioner experiences an initiation into a state of psychic empowerment, and expansive perception awareness.

Tantric yoga can be practiced individually, or with women and men in partners. The state of empowerment and awareness created within the Tantric practitioner is achieved through the process of inner heat and through the raising of the kundalini, the source of the inner heat.

Thus shamanic realization, which comes about through the arousal and movement of the kundalini, was attained by adepts in prehistoric times through the practices that we now know as

174

Tantra. Five thousand years ago in the Indus Valley, and nine thousand years ago in Old Europe, women and men consciously entwined their physical and spiritual energies in sexual union, and were able to direct their thoughts to bring about transformation within themselves, and in their environment. Empowered women and men made love and channeled the energy currents in their bodies, together impregnating the earth with their visions of growth and fertility.

This spiritual technology of women and men united in consciousness is the shamanic practice we need in the present time to alter the militaristic vibration on our planet into one that is life oriented and nourishing. Together we can infuse the earth with our love, with the potency of our deepest intention. Only empowered men and women can bring about a metamorphosis of consciousness.

As empowered women and men, in an exchange of spiritual transmissions, we can create a world to grow in, and raise our children in with our vision and with our love.

To bring together our spiritual power in present time, we must work to change present atrocities directed toward women, children and men. We must honor and educate each other with dignity and compassion. While either the female or male is hated there is only destructiveness, because the female and male contain the psychic and physical polarities that create the dance of generation, without which there is only degeneration and death.

As illuminated people in the present time, we can extract the positive transforming practices of the past, and leave the ignorance and errors behind. As vanguards in a revolution of spirit, we can become the light-bearers and the incarnation of the reality that we want most to manifest.

Shamanic consciousness

Shamanic awakening is a time of individuation, when the male and female principles of "I am" and Eros come together into an androgynous whole. The shaman is the expression of desire and love – the fire and union between man and woman.

The Goddess emerges from mythical time into a physical expression of her soul. She incarnates as the shamaness. Parashakti, the Goddess, the consort of experience, appears and moves from her belly, dancing until her head reaches her tail of consummation. Goddess of life, she moves from the dynamic flow of the serpent fire.

The shaman draws in the volcanic tides and gravitational pull of the earth, and floods her body with the seismic energy of the cosmos. Her life force courses through her into the world around her. She touches energy patterns and transforms according to the primal messages and DNA code of her body.

Her creativity emerges from the Tantric flow of her life. She sings and the world is created. She touches and the body and mind are made whole. From her passionate sucking in of life, she breathes out life.

Because of her freedom to move within the micro-macrocosm, she lives in universal time. She acts and moves with spontaneity and her creative acts are empowered by her inner world of orgasmic energy, by her own kundalini on fire.

Chapter 2

A personal vision of a shamanic community

I can imagine a shamanic community in which women and men celebrate the body and spirit in daily life, and in dance and ritual. The intention of the community is to help each individual become empowered by initiation into shamanic consciousness. That consciousness is a personal unfoldment of the mysteries of the inseparability of body and spirit.

I envision a community which encourages and nourishes values such as self-respect, esteem for others, and inter-cooperation. From what can be inferred from the archeological records, these were values highly regarded in the agricultural communities of Old Europe[2] and the Indus Valley.

A shamanic community can be created in the present time that brings together women and men in a unified spiritual technology. By design, the community helps each individual become empowered and successfully go through initiation into shamanic consciousness. As each initiate finds inner healing and experiences psychic wholeness, then the empowered one can in turn help other people who have not yet journeyed the path of inner clarity.

Shamanic ritual and transformation practices that lend themselves well to a community that is created intentionally for transformation can also be implemented in our present lifestyles, individually and among friends. The awareness created individually and collectively spirals concentrically outwards, touching others with consciousness and healing. Each person who moves with orgiastic health awakens a sympathetic response in our organic social and physical environment.

PHYSICAL ENVIRONMENT

To intentionally create a community that is nurturing and that is supportive of inner growth, it is important to select a physical environment that is conductive to transformation. The physical location needs to be aesthetically refreshing and rich in negative ions to induce physical and psychic restoration. Sited near a fresh source of water and an abundance of trees, the environment can facilitate in the residents the experience of emotional and psychic balance.

I envision an intentional community where there are centers of activity in which initiation and evolution into shamanic consciousness are possible. The initiation centers are like petals on a flower mandala:

- The matrix center of the community is the shaman's abode. The shaman serves as a compass to help guide the seekers to health and personal unfoldment. Within a beautiful, sunlit place, the shaman gives individualized meditation and healing practices to help each person who comes to achieve inner growth and balance.
- The healing center is built of redwood, stucco, or other natural materials, and is situated among wild flowers and trees. The naturopathic healers are there to provide psychic attunement and body balancing for those they work with. Directed by vision and guidance from the heart, the healers can help each client achieve a state of inner health and grace.
- The shamanic theater is a vortex for creative enactment of mythologies. Individual members have the opportunity to write their own mythologies and act them out. In the process of unearthing personal mythologies and images, and giving them psychic and ritualized energy, the creator of the script can find the source of personal shamanic power.
- The education center encompasses a school for healing and performing arts for children, where children learn to heal themselves and create their own rites of passage
- Primal religion is celebrated in the ritual center of the

community. At the designated power spot (one indoors, the other outdoors), members gather individually or collectively to enact rituals issuing from their own sacrality.

As the energies are interchanged within the centers, an alchemical synthesis can occur within the participant in the mandala community.

The matrix center

The empowered shaman in the community acts as the *axis mundi* — a compass for the seeker to find a direction to self-awareness. As the symbolic representative of the Goddess and God, where the shaman resides is a holy place. The shaman contains the unity — the meeting ground for heaven and earth.

3000 years ago in the Indus Valley, a tree marked the spot where the Goddess manifested.[3] The inner structure of the shaman's body has been compared to the structure of a tree. The spinal cord is the figurative trunk along which the kundalini travels from its origin at the base of the tree, to its final destination at the top of the tree, i.e. at the crown of the head.

Within the "sacred tree" of the shaman's spine, the shaman discovers the key to immortality. The tree or the body of the shaman, houses the power spot of illumination. In Old Europe and in the Indus Valley, artifacts indicate that the Goddess was often worshipped in the form of a tree spirit. Altars were often situated under a tree.[4]

What do these mean, these associations of goddess and tree, or goddess and vine . . . . They mean that here is a "Center of the World," that there is the source of life, youth and immortality. The tree signifies the universe in endless regeneration; but at the heart of the universe, there is always a tree — a tree of eternal life or knowledge.[5]

The seeker of personal power goes to the shaman to uncover her personal map of inner wisdom and power. The shaman can see the seeker's innate potential for wholeness and helps her reclaim lost parts of herself. The shaman works with the client to uncover forgotten dreams. To find clarity behind the client's blocks and obscurations, the shaman uses techniques to clear away blocks in energy centers of the body. The seeker may experience pressure or tightness in the throat area. Because the throat is the center of communication, the blocks may be due to the person withholding thoughts she wants to express, or the pressure in the throat may be due to someone directing thoughts of invalidation. For example, someone sends the negative thought to a woman that she as a woman should not speak authoritatively, or powerfully. The result might be that the woman receiving the thoughts feels a reserve, or constriction in the throat while communicating her thoughts or feelings. The way the shaman helps the client heal the throat constriction is by helping her to see her right to express her thoughts with a sense of her own power.

Shamans use different techniques to bring the client to the recognition of her own power, as Lynn Andrews described on p. 24:

> If I talk about the power held in the throat, I can teach how to let that energy go by making a throat bundle – doing something that is external and tangible to see what you are doing to yourself.

To receive into one's energy field other people's thoughts or energies, and to be strongly affected by the energies, is sometimes referred to as "possession." Whether or not the thought-forms were consciously sent out, or with the intention to do harm, the result is still that these thought-forms can cause obscurations for the person receiving them. The person who invalidates the self draws energy that is not nurturing or growth producing, feeding from other people's negativity by receptivity to it.

When the shaman removes blocks and foreign energies from a person's aura, she helps the individual draw back his or her own creative energy. The person's own energy source restores a balance to the body and psyche. Within each person's aura are the solutions to all of his or her questions.

The shaman can remove blocks and negative thought-forms by other methods as well, such as by elaborate ritual healing. By methods such as blowing or sucking out the harmful objects or thoughts, she can restore the client to a state of inner balance.

Another healing method that the shaman may employ is to fly in the spirit body to the astral world where the antagonists are sending the negative thought forms. The shaman can defeat the opponent and reclaim the energy that belongs to the client. When the energy is returned to her, the client who has been ill often experiences a reuniting with her "soul."

The contemporary shaman often uses transpersonal psychology and counseling as tools of empowerment. In a counseling session the shaman may ask the client to go on a journey for lost symbols and images that evoke power and direction. From the images that the client unearths from her world within, the shaman may work with her in a ritual that helps release the untapped energy.

The healing center

On the path of shamanic awakening, the initiate often experiences emotional pain when facing the depths of inner fears and traumas. In the process of personal metamorphosis, when the kundalini is stimulated, psychic and physical imbalances may arise. Special guidance, nurturance, and support are needed during those more fragile times.

In the transportive environment of the healing center, many restorative modalities can help facilitate harmony in the initiate. With natural diet, herbs, massage, chiropractic, homeopathy, acupuncture, and other physical approaches, the person can experience a comfort in the ground of his or her being. The body in harmony creates a support system for the mind and emotions. Music, flower scents, color lights, and toning return the senses and the subtle body to a state of tranquility.

Inner unfoldment and attunement are facilitated when the environment is composed of simple beauty. Within and outside the healing center, beautiful growing flowers and plants infuse the atmosphere with fragrance and color. In a fresh and vibrant atmosphere, the seeker can glimpse the rare depths of herself.

> Then taking two leaves, he laid them on his hands, and breathed on them and straightaway a living freshness filled the room, as if the air itself awoke and tingled sparkling with joy . . . for the fragrance that came to each of us was like a memory of dewy mornings, of unshadowed sun.[6]

The community healers act as catalysts for healing because they live out their own dreams. They possess heart because they have touched their own emotions deeply. Touching first their own hearts, the healers can touch those who are in pain, evoking light and peace. Healing work often centers around the heart, where emotions are stored. When feelings are released in an atmosphere of love and acceptance, healing begins.

A psychic healing administered by a shaman is one way a person can find renewal clarity and more physical well being. A community ritual healing is another way. The community healers can enter a trance dance and perform rites as their spirits instruct them. The healers may anoint the person with flower scents and massage him or her with oil. By whatever magic and process they use in the ritual, the healers touch the seeker. In trance they make contact with the transformative world of symbols and mythology.

In a shamanic community, and with special friends, sacred images can be explored that give power to one's life. There are many rituals that evoke the unconscious. For example:

> Lay down comfortably on the floor. Imagine yourself on a journey in a setting that makes you feel rapturous. Look around you at the beauty, and experience the transportive sensations within.
>
> In your mind put on ecstatic clothing, with soft, sensuous material. Allow yourself to reflect and play in that special place. Run through the waves of an ocean and allow yourself to be carried by the fizzing surf to the smooth shore. Sky dive from a cliff, feeling the air

pressure as you drop, and a lack of effort as you reach the soft turf below, and roll on the supportive earth.

Look around for an organic part of your environment that holds a lot of energy for you. If you experience a thrill spotting a delicate little shell along the beach, or when breaking open an oozing passion-fruit, that is your present. As you reflect on what the gift means to you, bring it back to your conscious life as a part of yourself you may have previously forgotten. Live out a positive fantasy in the ordinary world, letting your "find" guide you.

For example, if you bring back a feather from the Bird of Paradise, put some extravagantly beautiful colors into your wardrobe, and wear a feather as a talisman around your neck. Or if you come back with a pineapple from your imaginative voyage, do something that is sensual and exhilarating. Drink from the juice of your life.

There are many rituals to explore your inner images.

Crystal light

Sit together with a friend in a special space, with flowers in a bowl, candles and incense burning. Each wear beautiful light ceremonial clothing. Put the palms of your hands together with those of your friend and visualize crystal light pouring through your joined hands. Together, imagine the light streaming through your arms and spreading through your bodies until you both are flooded with light. In the quiet of visualization, imagine going within the crystal light of the mind, and look for an image that comes most clearly into focus. Each share your vision with the other, and then both breathe into the image, and sit together with your inner gifts until you both feel complete. Then each imagine your own symbol entering your heart, and validate its importance in your life.

Wooing the Spirit

Sit the seeker in the middle of a circle.
A group of healers play flutes, bells and chimes.
They decorate her hair with feathers and flowers,
garlands for her neck.
They paint her face with beautiful body make-up and glitter.
They sing songs and offer her fruit.
They coo and woo her spirit there to stay.

Iridescence

When you are tense and feeling contracted,
imagine dropping the armour around your heart.
See the heart as an opening to a rainbow-filled world
and walk inside.
Fill your heart up with iridescent colors.
Feel your heart become light and open
and then walk outside into the world again.

Rainbow transmission

In a circle of friends,
each person imagine a different hue
of the rainbow.
Mentally fill yourself up
with color
and release it as a shower
over the group.
Emerge from the rainbow shower
with a tingling sensation
of a fresh, clear aura.

Earth and sky

Sit on the earth under your tree of power.
Imagine an iridescent green snake
coming up from under the earth
under your anus

traveling up your spine.
Simultaneously
imagine a lightning bolt
flashing in the sky
entering the crown of your head
meeting the serpent
at your solar plexus.
Visualize the combined energies
of lightning and snake
returning up your spine
until the energy is released
in a firework display above your head
of flashing white and iridescent green.

Empowerment retreat

Women retreat together for a week-end and create rituals that express your womanliness. Dress as a chosen Goddess and create a ritual dance embodying her. Design a mask representing the aspect of the Goddess that you want to enact now in your life, and wear the mask as an embodiment of your power. Individually and collectively enact menses and childbirth rituals through mime and dance. As a closing, mentally project a vision into the universe with the power that is in your womb.

Men retreat together for a week-end, and create rituals that express your manliness. Dress as your favorite deity, and dance His dance. Design a mask representing the spirit of the God you want to embody and project His creative power into the world. Paint your bodies with war paint, and conquer the enemies within yourselves. Carve totems in the shape of your spirit allies, and offer them incense.

At the end of the week-end women and men come together. In a place of power, in a meadow, or around a fire, perform a ritual dance, wearing the deity masks and magical symbols of power.

The shamanic theater

With inner images and rituals brought to life, the seeker experiences nourishment. With the mythological material each person unearths about herself, the initiate is prepared to design a ritual to perform in the shamanic theater. By bringing herself into the open, the initiate will gain the full vision of her power. Like the shaman through antiquity, each person draws power into herself by acting out images from the spirit world, the unconscious, or the imagination (depending on his or her perspective).

Many millennia ago, the shaman enacted magic ritualistically. Theater was an integral part of women's sacrality in Old Europe. Molded figures with masks and large vases have been excavated on archaeological digs. The masks that have been found are incised and painted with various motifs, representing divinities, devotees, various animals, birds, and snakes. In Old Europe, theater, myth and the sacredness of personal transformation were all elements that were closely intertwined.

> Masks and masked figures, life-size or in miniature, of ancient Greece, Minoan Crete and Old Europe, imply liturgy and drama whose emphasis is theatrical. It is quite conceivable that all three belong to the same tradition. Masked figures are mimetic representations of rituals and mythological scenes.[7]

In Old Europe, theater was used as a means for self-unfoldment, and for magical effects in the environment. Sacred rites that produced fertility and growth in the crops were also rituals that gave the shaman woman freedom in astral flight, and dynamic energy as her serpent fire was stimulated. The symbolism of masks – such as the serpent and bird masks – represented transformation within women's shamanic tradition. Ritual theater was synonymous with spirituality.

The masked design was an early tradition of Southeastern Europe which was sustained through the millennia, and integral with the spiritual foundations of the society it nourished.[8]

Every actor is giving life to her own mythology when she dons a mask, and is transformed into a costumed character. Each actor is an enactment of her own divinity. The act of dramatizing is magically empowering. In ancient Greece this alchemical process was lived out in ritual, and was symbolically represented on personal artifacts.

On a Minoan ring from Phaistos (Webster 1959: 8, fig. 4) a human mask is shown between two gods. Portrayal of the mask alone was as important as portrayal of masked creatures, for it was the receptacle of invisible divine forces. The priests or priestesses and the worshippers of ancient Greece and Italy wore masks; the satyrs and the maenads who danced in frenzy at Dionysian festivals, were masked; everyone who danced for the god and made music was masked. Each different mythical persona was represented by a different mask.[9]

As a continuum in the tradition of sacred theater, the present day shamanic theater waters the seeds of our own transformation. The shamanic theater is a sacred center where we ritually enact visions and dreams. The stage can be outdoors in a grove of trees or indoors on a theater stage. The ingredients of the transformative theater are now as they have been for over 10,000 years: the shaman actors weave the intricacies of the inner self into an outer form; the audience forms a community; there are costumes, masks, and sets for changing the tone of the play.

As the actor acts out her reality, she is drawing from the power within, giving it life, and adding the impregnated facets of herself. The more fully the actor dramatizes her symbols and mythology, the more magic and transformation she creates within herself. The actor who fully invests herself in her work becomes the affirmation of herself . . . of life itself.

The theater is an ever-fluid mandala, changing in borders, contents, design, but always containing the essence of the woman or man. In the shamanic theater the actor writes her own songs, choreographs her own costumes and sets. The play is her own circle of power, drawn by her own hands.

Being witnessed as real, as authentic, is a key in shamanic healing. Feelings and emotions are seen and experienced by the community. The feeling of wholeness that the actor experiences comes from the validation that she has expressed herself in total, and has been seen in her totality by others. The circuit is complete. The inner images brought to life are simultaneously experienced by the actor and the community. The actor-initiate, realizing inner and outer validation, feels reintegrated into society. The transition is made from feeling fragmented or soulless to the realization of wholeness. With the fullness of self-love, the initiate embodies the health and grace of her self.

The education center

The children are the flowers of the community in all conscious and spiritual societies. Great care is given them so that they may grow with self-awareness, self-love, and compassion toward others. In the shamanic children's school, tools are given the children to experience empowerment and loving awareness. They learn to develop sensitivity to each other's needs and to nurture and heal one another.

In a shamanic school, the children have an opportunity to learn about and experience the multi-facets of the visual and performing arts. Both hemispheres of the brain are stimulated in a holistic learning environment. Using the shamanic paradigm as a model, children learn both the theoretical and the experiential when approaching any of the interrelated subjects taught at the school. In the theater arts, the children create their own plays and musical performances. Through the experience of drama, the children experience their creativity and are an integral part of the inner life of their peers. Each child learns to produce their own works, and thereby experiences the satisfaction of manifesting the whole creative process.

In a patriarchal system, children are taught that they are born powerless, and must compete with their peers for any attainment. The child then grows up and spends a lifetime seeking control of her or his life.

The child in a shamanic school learns at an early age that she or he is in charge of completion and of bringing creative projects into fruition without judgment, and without rejection. Self-empowerment and efficacy are within the child's control. At the same time the child is not alone, but is supported and nurtured by peers, and by adults in his or her world.

The children's dance

In a tree where they are fully visible, place a pair of female and male dolls in the branches. Decorate the "deities" with beautiful clothes, jewelry, flowers, and feathers. Below the dolls on a branch of the tree hang a low wooden swing.

As a community come together in a tree swinging celebration. Bedecked with flowers and garlands, dance around the "deity tree," taking turns in the center swinging. Shower the swinger with song and flowers, while holding hands in a circle. Together, chant something like:

"The Goddess in you, the Goddess in me I sing!
The God in me, the God in you I dance!"

Play the day away with feasting, and games. Before you leave at the end of the day, as an offering for the festivity, place something under the tree for the animals who live in the woods: some nuts . . . berries . . . a handful of seeds.

"To the Goddess in you, to the God in me I make this offering!"

The Ritual Center

The ritual center in the shamanic community is a space where the community members gather to celebrate and worship their relationship to the Primal. In the sacred space, a person worships the inner Self, and celebrates the creative forces of deities united within.

In prehistoric Old Europe, and in the Indus Valley cultures, the Goddess and God were celebrated and meditated upon. The conjugal union of the divine couple aroused ecstacy in the practitioners. Their tantric embrace was synonymous with new beginnings: fertility, children, verdant crops, fragrant flowers, and ecstacy.[10] Flowers were thrown in the air. Flowers were worn as garlands, and laced the hair of the woman shaman and her virile lover, the divine representatives. The hypnotic sound of sweet flutes, lyres, and pipes lingered in the air. Drums beat until dancers fell into the grass, full of the offered fruits, full of heady wine and the intoxication of music and celebration.

The Dravidian peoples who migrated from the Mediterranean arrived in the Indus Valley around 3000 BC.[11] They brought with them early forms of ritual from Old Europe, that dated back *c.* 7000 BC.[12] One of the forms of ritual celebration was *puja* – the offering of flowers to the Goddess and her Divine Consort.

> The characteristic ritual of puja is most likely Dravidian; the word itself is formed by joining pu (flower) with v je (to go; palatized to v je) to signify the flower ritual . . . .
> In the puja ritual a consecrated image or symbol is worshipped as a living personality, invoked and greeted with grateful offerings, waving of lights and singing of prayers. The offerings consist of leaves, flowers, fruits, water, etc.[13]

Women and men coming together and creating new mythologies in ritual can heal each other's wounds and become whole in relationship to one another. A ritual dramatization of new possibilities in relationship is an initiation into new creation. Together consciously choosing the ingredients of a new paradigm, we can enact the reality we want to create within a community. The potency of our acts moves out in concentrically widening circles.

The ritual center is a space that marks a unity of all the elements of primal religion. It is a mandala that unifies and connects the sacred threads of the feminine and masculine lineages of spirituality from the prehistoric to the present. The shamanic paradigm is a cyclical one. It will continue to revolve and channel the essence of the divine polarities as long as there is creation to manifest those energies. In the embrace of the Goddess and God the world is conceived and born, dissolved and reborn.

Ritual and visualization is the creative wheel that moves through time and space, creating new forms and new realities.

A lover's ritual

Lovers meet in a sacred space
surrounded by growing plants, flowers, and bush.
While in conjugal embrace
experience
a primordial world
shimmering, fresh, and beautiful.
In your love-making
give your partner the most ecstatic
vision you can conceive.
When consummated and full
of love, touch, and juice,
offer your partner a flower
or a dew drop on a leaf
and know that your vision
is healing the world.

Within the sacred centers of the new shamanic community there is a celebration of women and men who live out their mythologies and are inseminated with more life.

Within each center there is space and nourishment for the children.

Within each center there is healing, and growth, as old concepts fall away and freshness penetrates the body, mind, and spirit.

Within each center there is a womb that contains energies that are dynamic and contain the seeds for birth.

SACRED DREAMS

Between Goddess and God
there is no separation
But eternally fused in transportive
               dance
               their touch
               their breath
               their smile
               is one.
In their embrace   they create
               universes.
Between you and I there is no separation
               I feel you
               in me
               on me
               and around me.
Together
we are conceiving
infinite dreams

in our minds

Appendix
A ritualized play

A ritualized play can be an enactment of a dream, a fantasy, or may involve a person's relationship to the primary themes of life, such as the themes of birth, death, and rebirth. As an example of a ritualized play, here are some excerpts from my play entitled *The Mother is Burning*.

The stage is dark as the narrator reads the opening lines of *The Mother is Burning*. The narrator's voice is deep and resonant.

THE MOTHER IS BURNING

the moon rose on a shadowy hill
woman's blues in the air
Shalimar felt the dampness as it dripped
down her cheeks.
her lips felt hard
the night red
a scorching dripping night.
she breathed sultry music
from ginger flowers
and smelled the sulphur
of a burning mountain.
Shalimar let out a wail
from her heart searing hot
. . . the mother was burning
her heart dripping lava
the earth soaked up her cries
and heaved

the rage and pain
breaking it open.
the moon hid from the sky
. . . woman's blues in the air

Shalimar lifted her head to listen
as a panther murmured in the bushes
but it was only a night spirit whispering
. . . Your man is dead.

SCENE 1

The lights come up dimly on a funeral scene. Center stage
there is an oak coffin. About twenty-four people with gray
cloaks and hoods move in a circle around the coffin. As each
person looks in the coffin and rejoins the circle, a woman
initiates a chant, while one of the members plays a conga.
   "He is gone into the night . . . warrior of the night . . .
alone . . . alone . . . he will live in the night of the people . . .
today he's gone alone . . . alone into the night . . . alone . . .
alone . . ."
   The lights dim to black-out while the chant continues.
   Misty grey lights come up on a woman. She too is dressed in
a gray cloak with a hood. In dreamlike movement she is
carrying a man's corpse back and forth across the room. In the
background the voices are chanting, "Alone . . . alone . . .
warrior of the night . . . he is gone into the night . . . alone
. . ." The woman continues her procession with the corpse
while the mist thickens. Black-out.

SCENE 2

Lights come up on the woman. She is naked, her body painted
red. On her head is a head-dress of scarlet feathers, around her
ankles are bands of shells. She is holding a small baby in a sling
at her breast and is standing facing the audience. She looks out
at the people and asks them, "What is *death*? . . ." After a long

silence she says, "In this world death is a denial. In the next –
death is a journey between worlds."

After a pause she stoops down and dips her hand into a
gourd filled with milk, saying "*Life* is Vision . . . in this world
and in the next. . . ." She then sprays the milk at the audience,
saying, "Suckle your life. . . ."

She then joins the circle of women and men who are softly
beating congas and singing a song that is slow and melodic.
Reverberating chants continue until a hypnotic atmosphere is
tangible. The woman of red silently hands her baby to one of
the other women, and reaches her hand again into the gourd of
milk. She anoints each woman's and man's head, saying to
each one. "Your life . . ." Then she dips her hand into a pot of
ashes and rubs ashes on each person's head, saying, "Your
death . . ." Then she puts her hand into a third vessel and
anoints each head with red clay, saying, "Your rebirth . . ."

The woman anoints her own head with white, black and red.
A woman and man sitting in the circle beat the congas as
everyone chants, "We live, we die, we are reborn . . . we live,
we die, we awaken . . ."

After several minutes, the red woman slips out of the
chanting circle, and gathers up a feather cape that is lying on
the floor. She encloaks herself in the white, black and red
feathered cape. The lights become filmy grey. There is still the
discernible sound of chanting. The red woman is no longer
seen, but there is the sound of wings, and a tinkling of shells.

The lights come up on the woman leaning over a body on the
ground. The lights give the illusion of gray fog swirling
around the two figures. The woman takes two sticks from the
ground and rubs them, creating a fire. From the charred sticks
she takes black ashes and smears them on the dead man's head.
As she anoints him she says, "From your death there is
rebirth." She then takes ointments out of the bag she has been
carrying and smears white and red clay on his cheeks. Behind
them the fire burns with intensity. The fire creates a color play
and shadows the man and woman's cheeks. Breathing is heard
as the dead man's body begins undulating with each breath.
The woman bends over him and begins synchronizing her

movements with him. He opens his eyes slowly, and they
continue moving with continuous eye contact. They move
deeper into a ⸜sexual dance, shaking their bodies with the
energy flow, and writhing on the floor together as the fire
blazes red. All that is heard is the sound of their breathing and
the tinkle of the shells on the woman's ankles.

After many minutes the faint sound of drumbeat becomes
audible, and the blaze of the fire ebbs. Slowly their sexual
dance comes to a stop.

The woman and man both stand and walk over to the now
dimly lit fire.

They sit in silence, feeling the extraordinariness of their
reunion. Then she looks suddenly as though she has wakened
from trance. As she speaks again, her voice shakes.

"Even though I know we are inseparable in spirit, when you
left your body, my world collapsed. Every night I carried your
corpse in my dreams. If there was a way I could have guarded
you from your destroyers – but there wasn't a way."

The man nods, looking at her with pain in his eyes, and
reaches out to hold her.

After a time a baby's cry is heard in the background. The red
woman looks as though she must depart. She takes a little bag
from around her neck, and puts it into the palms of the man's
hands, saying, "There is something inside to remind you that
we are both free to travel between our worlds.

The man takes out two small clay sculptures: one of a bird
woman, the other of a bird man. He kisses her and whispers,
"In life, in death, and in rebirth we will meet."

The woman takes a flask and a bag of seeds from her cape.
She sprinkles white fluid and seeds into his hands.

As he drinks of it from her hands, she whispers, "From my
womb you will awaken."
Black-out. All that is heard is the tinkling of shells.

Dim lights come up on the circle of men and women, one of
whom is holding the softly crying baby. They are sitting in
candlelight. The red woman re-enters the room, removing her
cape. She sits down in the circle, taking her baby who
immediately begins to nurse, and make loud sucking sounds.

The group begins a soft lullaby, while one man plays the flute, and one woman plays the conga.

> Veil light
> O veil light comes with a hush
> that beds the evening
> and cloaks the thrush
> who start off their journey
> on a soft weathered flight
> into the veil light
> into the veil light . . .

Black-out.

Notes

PREFACE

1 Marija Gimbutas, *The Gods and Goddesses of Old Europe*, Berkeley, University of California Press, 1982, pp.144–5.

PART I: *INTRODUCTION*

1 Joan Halifax, *Shamanic Voices*, New York, E.P. Dutton, 1979, p.3. Mircea Eliade, *Patterns in Comparative Religion*, New York, Sheed & Ward, Inc., 1958, pp.85–6.
2 Gopi Krishna, *The Awakening of the Kundalini*, New York, E.P. Dutton, 1975, p.17.
3 Marija Gimbutas, "Woman and culture in goddess oriented Old Europe," an article from the anthology: *The Politics of Women's Spirituality*, edited by Charlene Spretnak, New York, Doubleday, 1982, p.23.
4 Mircea Eliade, *A History of Religious Ideas*, Chicago, University of Chicago Press, 1978, p.46.
5 Marija Gimbutas, *The Goddesses and Gods of Old Europe*, Berkeley, University of California Press, p.i, Preface.
   Arthur Basham, *The Wonder that was India*, New York, Taplinger Press Publishing Co., 1967, pp.29, 30.
   Narendra Nath Bhattacharya, *The History of Śakta Hinduism*, New Delhi, India, Munshiram, Mansharlal Pub. Ltd, 1974, pp. 20–21.
6 Marija Gimbutas, op. cit., p.30.
7 *The King James Bible*, Genesis 1: 26.

198

PART III: *THE NEW SHAMANIC COMMUNITY*

1 H. Zimmer, *Philosophies of India*, New York, Pantheon Books, 1951, p.62.
2 See note 3, Introduction.
3 Arthur Basham, *The Wonder that was India*, New York, Taplinger Press, 1967, p.24.
4 See note 3, Introduction.
5 Mircea Eliade, *Patterns in Comparative Religion*, New York, Sheed and Ward, 1958, p. 289.
6 J.R.R. Tolkien, *The Return of the King*, New York, Ballantine Books, 1965, p.173.
7 Marija Gimbutas, *The Goddesses and Gods of Old Europe*, Berkeley, University of California Press, 1982, p.66.
8 Ibid., p.61.
9 Ibid., p.66.
10 Narenda Nath Bhattacharya in a work edited by D. Sircar, *The Śakta Cult and Tara*, Calcutta, India, University of Calcutta, 1967, p.143.
11 Narendra Nath Bhattacharya, *The History of Śakta Religion*, New Delhi, India, Munshiram, Mansharial Pub. Ltd, 1974, p.19.
12 Ibid., pp.20 21.
13 L. Gopal, "Non-Aryan Contributions To Indian Culture," an article contained in a collection of essays from: *Proceedings of the International Symposium on Ethnic Problems of Ancient History of Central Asia (Second Millennium BC)*, Dushanbe, 1977.

Select Bibliography

Allchin & Allchin, B., *The Birth of Indian Civilization*, Penguin Books, New York, 1972.

Allione, Tsultrim, *Women of Wisdom*, Routledge & Kegan Paul, London, 1984.

Andrews, Lynn, *Medicine Woman*, Harper & Row, San Francisco, 1981.
Flight of the Seventh Moon, Harper & Row, San Francisco, 1984.
Jaguar Woman, Harper & Row, San Francisco, 1985.

Arguelles, Jose, *Mandala*, Shambhala, Berkeley, 1972.

Basham, Arthur, *The Wonder that was India*, Taplinger Press Pub. Co., New York, 1967.

Beane, Wendell, *Myth, Cult, and Symbols in Śakta Hinduism*, E.J. Brill, Leiden, Netherlands, 1977.

Berreman, Gerald, *Caste and Other Inequities – Essays on Inequality*, Folklore Institute, Meerut, India, 1979.

Bhattacharya, Narendra Nath, *The History of Śakta Religion*, Munshiram Mansharlal Pub. Ltd, New Delhi, India, 1974.
The Indian Mother Goddess, New Delhi, 1977.

Briffault, Robert, *The Mothers*, George Allen & Unwin, London, 1959.

Brownman & Schwartz, *Spirits, Shamans and the Stars*, Nouton, New York, 1979.

Chatterji, S.K., *Indo-Aryan and Hindi*, Firma K.L. Mukhopadhyaya, Calcutta, India, 1960.

Childe, Gordon, *What Happened in History*, Penguin Books, New York, 1942.

Christ, Carol, and Plaskow, Judith, *Woman Spirit Rising*, Harper & Row, San Francisco, 1979.

Crookall, Robert, *Ecstacy – The Release of the Soul from the Body*, Darshana Printers, Moradadad, India, 1973.

Deetz, James, *Invitation to Archaeology*, Natural History Press, New York, 1967.

Edsman, Carl, *Studies in Shamanism*, Almquist and Wiksalls, Boltackeri, A.B., 1967.

200

Eliade, Mircea, *Birth and Rebirth*, Harper & Row, New York, 1958.
Patterns in Comparative Religion, Sheed and Wared, Inc., New York, 1958.
Shamanism – Archaic Techniques of Ecstacy, Princeton University Press, Princeton, New Yersey, 1964.
Yoga, Freedom and Immortality, Princeton University Press for the Bollingen Foundation, New Jersey, 1969.
A History of Religious Ideas, Volume 1, University of Chicago Press, Chicago, 1978.
Fagan, Brian, *Avenues of Antiquity*, W.H. Freeman and Co., San Francisco, 1959.
Fairservis, Walter, *The Harappan Civilization – More Evidence, More Theory*, Aris & Phillips, England, 1959.
Falk, Nancy, *Unspoken Worlds: Women's Religious Lives in Non-Western Cultures*, Harper & Row, San Francisco, 1980.
Fisher, E., *Women's Creation: Sexual Evolution and the Shaping of Our Society*, Doubleday, New York, 1979.
Frazer, James, *Myths of the Origin of Fire*, Hacker Art Books (reissued), New York, 1974.
Gimbutas, Marija, *The Goddesses and Gods of Old Europe*, University of California Press, Berkeley and Los Angeles, 1982.
"The Temples of Old Europe," *Archaeology*, Nov./Dec. 1980, pp.11–50.
"Women and Culture in Goddess-Oriented Old Europe," *The Politics of Women's Spirituality*, Doubleday, New York, 1982.
Gopal, L., "Non-Aryan Contributions to Indian Culture," *Proceedings of the International Symposium on Ethnic Problems of Ancient History of Central Asia – (Second Millenium BC)*, Dushanbe, 1977.
Gopi Krishna, *The Awakening of the Kundalini*, E.P. Dutton, New York 1975.
Gough, Katharine, *The Origins of the Family*, Hogtown Press, Publication 44, New York, 1972.
Halifax, Joan, *Shamanic Voices*, E.P. Dutton, New York, 1979.
Shaman: Wounded Healer, Crossroad, New York, 1982.
Harner, Michael, *Way of the Shaman: A Guide to Power and Healing*, Harper & Row, San Francisco, 1980.
Heinze, Ruth-Inge, "The Nature and Function of Some Therapeutic Techniques in Thailand," *Asian Folklore Studies*, 2, 1977, pp.85–104.
(translator and commentator) *The Biography of Ahjan Man*, Taipei; Asian Folklore and Social Life Monograph 89, 1977.
The Role of the Sangha in Modern Thailand, Taipei; Asian Folklore and Social Life Monograph 93, 1977.
"Mediumship in Singapore Today," *Journal of Sociology and Psychology*, 2, 1979, pp. 54–70.
"The Social Implications of the Relationships Between Mediums, Entourage and Clients in Singapore Today," *Southeast Asian Journal*

of Social Sciences, VII:2, 1979, pp.60–80.

"Glossolalia in Singapore," *Folklore* VII, January 1982, pp.33–8.

"Shamans or Mediums, Toward a Definition of Different States of Consciousness," *Phoenix: Journal of Transpersonal Anthropology*, VI:1–2, 1982, pp.25–44.

Tham Khwan – How to Contain the Essence of Life: A Socio-Psychological Comparison of a Thai Custom, Singapore, Singapore University Press, 1982.

"Automatic Writing in Singapore," *Contributions to Southeast Asian Ethnography*, 2, August 1983, pp.146–60.

(ed.) *Proceedings of the First International Conference on the Study of Shamanism*, Berkeley, Independent Scholars of Asia, 1984.

(ed.) *Proceedings of the Conference on the Art of Healing*, Berkeley, Independent Scholars of Asia, 1985.

(ed.) *Proceedings of the Second International Conference on the Study of Shamanism*, Berkeley, Independent Scholars of Asia, 1985.

"Consciousness and Self-Deception: The Art of Undeceiving," *Saybrook Review*, vol.5, no.2, Fall/Winter 1985, pp.11–27.

Hunt, Roland, *The Seven Keys to Color Healing*, C.W. Daniel, London, 1973.

Jamal, Michele, *"Fertility," California State University of Long Beach Poetry Anthology*, Long Beach, 1970, p.2.

"Shamaness Religion," Journal of Women and Religion, vol.1, no.1, Graduate Theological Union, Spring 1981, Berkeley, p.13.

"The Sacred Fire," Psi Research Journal, San Francisco, June 1985, p.110.

"The Kundalini Fire: A Key to Healing," *Psi Research Journal*, San Francisco, September/December 1985, p.222.

Lame Deer, *Lame Deer – Seeker of Visions*, Simon and Schuster, New York, 1972.

Larsen, Steven, *The Shaman's Doorway*, Harper & Row, New York, 1976.

Leadbeater, C.W., *The Chakras*, The Theosophical Publishing House, Illinois, 1980.

Leroi-Gourhan, Andre, "The Evolution of Palaeolithic Art", from *Avenues of Antiquity*, W.H. Freeman & Co., San Francisco, 1959.

Liebert, Gosta, *Iconographic Dictionary of the Indian Religions*, E.J. Brill, Leiden, 1976.

Mann, Edward, *Orgone, Reich and Eros*, Simon and Schuster, New York, 1973.

Marshall, James, *Taxila*, Orient Book Distributor, Livingston, New Jersey, 1975.

Mellart, James, *Earliest Civilizations in the Near East*, McGraw Hill, New York, 1965.

Mookerjee, Ajitcoomar, *Kundalini – The Arousal of the Inner Energy*, Destiny Books, New York, 1982.

Morgan, Lewis Henry, *Ancient Society*, Belknap Press, Cambridge, Massachusetts, 1964.

Mundkur, Balajii, *The Cult of the Serpent*, Harvard University Press, Albany, New York, 1983.

Murray, Margaret, *The Genesis of Religion*, Routledge & Kegan Paul, London, 1963.

Noble, Vicki, *Motherpeace*, Harper & Row, San Francisco, 1983.

Ochahorn, J., *The Female Experience and the Nature of the Divine*, Indiana University Press, Bloomington, Indiana, 1981.

Pattee, Rowena, *Song to Thee: Divine Androgyne*, Celestial Arts, Mill Valley, 1973.
Moving with Change: A Woman's Reintegration of the I Ching, Routledge & Kegan Paul, London, 1986.

Prakash, B., *Rig Veda and the Indus Valley Civilization*, Vishveshvaranand Institute, New Delhi, 1966.

Preston, James, *Mother Worship*, University of North Carolina Press, Chapel Hill, 1981.

Sannella, Lee, *Kundalini – Transcendence or Psychosis?*, H.S. Dakin Company, San Francisco, 1976.

Sircar, Dineschandra, *The Śakti Cult and Tara*, University of Calcutta, Calcutta, India, 1967.

Spretnak, Charlene, *Lost Goddesses of Ancient Greece: A Collection of Pre-Hollenic Mythology*, Moon Books, Berkeley, 1978.
The Politics of Women's Spirituality, Doubleday, New York, 1982.

Stevens, Petey, *Opening Up to Your Psychic Self – A Psychic Primer*, Never-the-less Press, Berkeley, 1983.

Teish, Luisah, *Jambalaya: The Natural Woman's Book of Personal Charms and Practical Rituals*, Harper & Row, San Francisco, 1985.

Tolkien, J.R.R., *The Return of the King*, Ballantine Books, New York, 1965.

Valadez, Susana, "Huichol Women's Art," *Art of the Huichol Indians*, The Fine Arts Museums of San Francisco/Harry N. Abrams, Inc., Publishers, New York, 1978.

Vequad, Yves, *The Women Painters of Mithila*, Thames and Hudson, London, 1977.

Vilenskaya, L., "Glowing Phantoms," *The ESP Papers*, S. Ostrander & L. Schroder, eds., New York, Bantam Books, 1976, pp.173–80. (Translated from Russian; originally published in *Tekhnika-Molodezhi*, no.10, 1974.)
"Microphenomena or Macrophenomena? Meeting Greater Challenges," *Psi Research* (San Francisco, CA), vol.3, no.1, March 1984, pp.98–112.

"Psi Research in the Soviet Union: Are They Ahead of Us –
Epilogue," in R. Targ & K. Harary, *The Mind Race: Understanding
and Using Psychic Abilities*, New York, Villard Books, 1984,
pp.247–60.

"Firewalking: A New Fad, A Scientific Riddle, or an Excellent Tool
for Healing, Spiritual Growth and Psychological Development?" *Psi
Research*, vol.3, no.2, June 1984, pp.102–18.

"Firewalking: Renewing an Old Tradition to Raise Consciousness,"
in R.-I. Heinze, ed., *Proceedings of the Second International Conference
on Shamanism*, Berkeley, Center for South and Southeast Asia
Studies, University of California, 1985, pp. 58-65.

"Firewalking and Beyond," *Psi Research*, vol.4, no.2, June 1985,
pp.91–109.

Vilenskaya, L. & Steffy, J., "Some Comparisons of Psychic Healing in
the USSR, Eastern and Western Europe, North America, China and
Brazil," *Psi Research*, vol.3, no.2, June 1984, pp.29–52.

Vogel, J., *Indian Serpent Lore, or the Nagas in Hindu Legend and Art*,
Indological Book House, Delhi, India, 1976.

Wallace, A., *The Death and Rebirth of the Seneca*, Random House, New
York, 1969.

Wheeler, Sir Robert Mortimer, *The Cambridge History of India*,
Cambridge University Press, Cambridge, England, 1922.

White, J., *Kundalini, Evolution and Enlightenment*, Doubleday, New
York, 1979.

Wood, E., *Yoga Dictionary*, Philosophical Society, New York, 1956.

Wooley, L., *A Forgotten Kingdom*, Penguin, London, 1954.

Zimmer, H., *Philosophies of India*, Pantheon Books, New York, 1951.